KEY

CONSTITUTIONAL
AND
ADMINISTRATIVE LAW

2009–2010 EDITION

JOANNE SELLICK
WITH JANE REYNOLDS

HODDER
EDUCATION
AN HACHETTE UK COMPANY

Orders: please contact Bookpoint Ltd, 130 Milton Park, Abingdon, Oxon OX14 4SB.
Telephone: (44) 01235 827720. Fax: (44) 01235 400454. Lines are open from 9.00 -
5.00, Monday to Saturday, with a 24 hour message answering service. You can also order
through our website www.hoddereducation.co.uk

If you have any comments to make about this, or any of our other titles, please send them
to educationenquiries@hodder.co.uk

British Library Cataloguing in Publication Data
A catalogue record for this title is available from the British Library

ISBN: 978 0 340 98585 4

First Edition Published 2003
Second Edition Published 2006
This Edition Published 2009
Impression number   10 9 8 7 6 5 4 3 2 1
Year   2013 2012 2011 2010 2009

Copyright © 2009 Joanne Sellick, Jane Reynolds

Hachette UK's policy is to use papers that are natural, renewable and recyclable products
and made from wood grown in sustainable forests. The logging and manufacturing
processes are expected to conform to the environmental regulations of the country of origin.

Typeset by Transet Limited, Coventry, Warwickshire
Printed in Great Britain for Hodder Education, an Hachette UK Company, 338 Euston
Road, London NW1 3BH by Cox & Wyman Ltd, Reading, Berkshire

Contents

Preface

The Key Facts series is designed to give a clear view of each subject. This will be useful to students when tackling new topics and is invaluable as a revision aid. Most chapters open with an outline in diagram form of the points covered in that chapter. The points are then developed in list form to make learning easier. Supporting cases are given throughout by name and for some complex areas the facts of cases are given to reinforce the point being made.

The topics covered for Constitutional and Administrative Law are suitable for students studying on a variety of courses, especially first year degree and foundation courses in law. This book includes chapters on the nature of constitutions, sources of constitutional law, fundamental doctrines, Parliament and central government, the implications of membership of the European Union, civil liberties (including public order and police powers), human rights (with reference to the European Convention on Human Rights and the Human Rights Act 1998) and judicial review.

The law is as we believe it to be on 1st January 2009.

CHAPTER 1

Introductory matters

1.1 What is a constitution?

1. A basic definition of a 'constitution' would be a body of rules regulating the way in which an organisation or institution operates. However, when the term 'constitution' is used in the context of a State's constitution the definition is a little more complex.
2. The constitution of a State would be expected to:
   - establish the organs of government. Traditionally, this would consist of a body responsible for legislative functions; a body responsible for executive functions; and a body responsible for judicial functions;
   - allocate power between those institutions;
   - provide for the resolution of disputes on the interpretation of the constitution;
   - establish procedures etc. for the amendment of the constitution.
3. The constitution therefore defines the relationship between the various institutions of the State (horizontal relationship) and that between the State and the individual (vertical relationship).
4. In a narrow sense, a constitution could be defined as a particular document (or series of documents) setting out the framework and principal functions of the organs of government in a particular State. Such a constitution will have, as Wade describes, 'special legal sanctity', meaning that it is the highest form of law in the State.
5. The majority of States have such a constitution, against which all other laws are measured. Should such laws fail to conform to the constitution, they may be declared unconstitutional by the courts.
6. The United Kingdom does not have a constitution that is the highest form of law since its constitutional principles

can be amended by the passing of ordinary legislation – a consequence of the principle known as parliamentary supremacy (discussed in Chapter 4).

7. For this reason some have argued that the United Kingdom does not have a constitution. However, if we consider the wider definition of a constitution, which would be one that refers to the whole system of government, including all the laws and rules that regulate that government, we can clearly see that the United Kingdom does have a constitution.

1.2 The classification of constitutions

Constitutions can be classified in a number of different ways.

Codified (written) or uncodified (unwritten)

1. This has been the traditional way of classifying a constitution. In many examples, constitutions are described as being written or unwritten. This is too simplistic an explanation. It is more accurate to describe constitutions as codified or uncodified.

2. A **codified** constitution is one where the constitution is enshrined in a single document or series of documents, as, for example, in the United States of America.

3. An **uncodified** constitution is one where the constitutional rules exist, and indeed may be written down in legislation, but there is no one source that can be identified.

4. The United Kingdom is the only major country in the world not to have a codified constitution. Consequently, the sources of the UK constitution are varied and include, for example, statute, common law and conventions. (The sources of the UK constitution are discussed in Chapter 2.)

5. In modern constitutional terms the desire to create a codified constitution will often be the result of some significant event, such as, for example:
   - revolution (e.g. France 1789);

- reconstruction and/or redefinition of a State's institutions following war/armed conflict (e.g. Germany, Iraq);
- conferment of independence on a former colony (e.g. India, Australia, Canada);
- creation of a new State by the union of formerly independent States (e.g. United States of America, Malaysia);
- creation of a new State(s) by the break up of a former Union of States (e.g. States created by the break up of the former Republic of Yugoslavia).

6. The United Kingdom has suffered no major historical or political event that has necessitated the creation of a codified constitution. There have nevertheless been significant constitutional events such as for example the:
   - 1688 Revolution;
   - union of England and Scotland (1707) and Great Britain with Ireland (1800);
   - House of Lords crisis 1910;
   - abdication of the monarch 1936; and
   - joining the European Economic Community in 1973.

   However, all of these events were dealt with by the passing of ordinary legislation such as, for example, the:
   - Bill of Rights 1688/9;
   - Parliament Act 1911;
   - Abdication Act 1936; and
   - European Communities Act 1972.

   Hence the United Kingdom's constitution has **evolved** over time and remains uncodified.

Rigid or flexible

1. This way of classifying a constitution was first suggested by Lord Bryce in the late 19th century.
2. A **flexible** constitution is one where all the laws of that constitution may be amended by the ordinary law-making process. The UK has a flexible constitution.

3. A **rigid** constitution is one where the laws of that constitution can only be amended by special procedures. Consequently, the constitution is '**entrenched**'. In other words, it is protected from being changed by the need to comply with a special procedure.

4. For example, the United States has a rigid constitution that cannot be amended by the passing of an ordinary piece of legislation (an Act of Congress). A special procedure has to be followed, which requires there to be:
   - a two-thirds majority in each House of the Federal Congress (the legislative body), followed by:
   - the acceptance (ratification) of at least three-quarters of the individual states that make up the United States.

5. In the Republic of Ireland, a Bill passed by both Houses of Parliament, a majority of votes in a referendum and the assent of the President are required to change the constitution.

Unitary or federal

1. A **federal** constitution is one where government powers are divided between central (federal) organs and the organs of the individual states/provinces that make up the federation. For example, the United States of America and Canada have federal constitutions. If there is to be any change in the distribution of power between the federal organs and the state organs, there must be amendment of the constitution using a special procedure.

2. A **unitary** constitution is one where all government power rests in the hands of one central set of organs.

Other classifications

A number of constitutional experts have identified other ways in which constitutions can be classified. For example:

1. Constitutions can be described as being:
   - **Supreme or subordinate** – if the legislature cannot change the constitution by itself, then the constitution is

supreme. If the legislature can change the constitution by itself, then it is **subordinate**.

- **Monarchical or republican**:
  - (a) in a monarchical constitution, the Head of State is a King or Queen and State powers are exercised in their name.
  - (b) In a republican constitution, the Head of State is a President.
  - (c) This classification has become less popular since the majority of monarchies, including the United Kingdom, have, in practical terms, removed the constitutional power of the Monarch.
  - (d) In the United Kingdom, for example, the majority power rests with Parliament and the executive.
  - (e) In contrast, in a republican constitution, such as the USA, the Head of State, the President, has significantly more power since they are elected and consequently accountable to the people.

- **Fused or separated** – the latter is a constitution that adheres to the doctrine of the separation of powers. The former is one that does not, so that certain organs of the State have a range of powers. (The separation of powers is discussed in Chapter 3.)

2. De Smith claims that constitutions can also be classified as **presidential** (e.g. the United States) or **parliamentary** (e.g. the United Kingdom).
   - (a) In a **parliamentary** system the people choose representatives to form the legislature. The legislature will be responsible for scrutinising the executive and consenting to laws. There is usually a separate Head of State who formally and ceremonially represents the State but who has little political power.
   - (b) In a **presidential** system the leader of the executive, the President, is elected independently of the legislature. The President appoints the rest of the executive, who are often not members of the legislature. The President is also the Head of State.

1.3 The United Kingdom's constitution

The key aspects of the United Kingdom's constitution can be classified as:

- **Uncodified (or unwritten)** – The United Kingdom does not have a codified constitution since there is no single document or series of documents that contain the constitution.
- **Unitary** – The United Kingdom is a union of once separate countries but operates a unitary rather than federal system. The Parliament, sitting at Westminster, has full legislative supremacy but has granted considerable self-government through the process of **devolution** to Scotland (Scotland Act 1998), Northern Ireland (Northern Ireland Act 1998) and Wales (Wales Act 1998). However, the arrangements preserve the unlimited power of Parliament to legislate for the devolved regions and to override laws made by any of the devolved bodies. Numerous matters remain outside the authority of the devolved bodies to legislate on: for example, international relations, defence and national security, economic and fiscal policies are reserved matters under the Scotland Act 1998. In addition, Parliament retains the authority to repeal these Acts and regain power to fully govern (see Chapter 4).
- **Flexible** – The constitution is flexible because all laws relating to it can be enacted, repealed and/or amended by Parliament using the same procedure, i.e. the passing of an ordinary Act of Parliament. There is no superior form of law or entrenchment.
- **Monarchical** – The Queen is the Head of State and succession to the throne is based on the hereditary principle. However, by convention (see Chapter 2) the Queen exercises her constitutional powers only on the advice of her Ministers and, in many cases, the powers are in fact exercised by Ministers in her name.

- **Parliamentary supremacy** – Parliament is supreme and can make or unmake any law and legislate on anything it wishes. In theory, no Parliament can be bound by its predecessors or bind its successors. (This principle and the limitations now imposed on it by, for example, membership of the European Union are discussed in detail in Chapters 4 and 8.)
- **Bicameralist** – The United Kingdom has a legislative body known as Parliament, which is composed of two chambers (see Chapter 5). These two chambers are known as the House of Commons (the lower House) and the House of Lords (the upper House).
- **Democratic** – The House of Commons has a membership that is directly elected at least every five years. The political party that wins the majority of seats in the House makes up the Government. The leader of that political party is then appointed by the Queen to be the Prime Minister, who in turn nominates the Ministers of the Government who are responsible for departmental activities and accountable to Parliament. (The electoral system is discussed in detail in Chapter 5.)

1.4 The advantages and disadvantages of codifying the United Kingdom's constitution

1. The advantages of an uncodified constitution such as that of the United Kingdom include the following:
   - the constitution is flexible and easily adaptable to change; and
   - Dicey argued that the United Kingdom's constitution was one embedded in the structure of the law as a whole, rather than being merely a piece of paper that could be destroyed.
2. The disadvantages of an uncodified constitution include the following:

- because of the flexibility of the constitution, constitutional principles can change without the support of the people;
- the ease with which the constitution can change can lead to confusion and people are left unsure of the constitutional position;
- the lack of a codified constitution means that many people do not know or understand constitutional principles; and
- the courts cannot declare Acts of Parliament to be unconstitutional.

3. Since the election of the Labour Government in 1997 the United Kingdom's constitution has undergone the most far-reaching reform since the 19th century. The reforms, whilst not all necessarily completed (e.g. reform of the House of Lords), could be moving the United Kingdom away from the traditional unitary state with an unwritten constitution and a sovereign parliament. For example:

- the **constitution is increasingly being reduced to writing/codified**. In 2004 Lord Bingham identified 18 statutes of constitutional importance that had been introduced since 1997;
- the **doctrine of parliamentary supremacy has been modified** by the supremacy of European Community law (see Chapter 8) and the incorporation of the European Convention on Human Rights by the Human Rights Act 1998 (see Chapter 9). In the context of the effect of membership of the European Union on the supremacy of Parliament, we can see a distinct modification of the traditional doctrine in that implied repeal no longer operates for certain important statutes. These have been called 'constitutional statutes' (see Chapters 2 and 4 for further discussion);
- the **Constitutional Reform Act 2005** provides for moves towards a more formal separation of executive, legislative and judicial powers (see Chapter 3);
- the process of **devolution** for Scotland, Wales and

Northern Ireland, whilst not formally affecting the unitary character of the constitution, has created a system that the sovereign Westminster Parliament is unable to undo in practice (see Chapter 4).

4. In conclusion, whilst it may be argued that a codified constitution would ensure that important principles are consented to by the people, enshrined and subject to change only when approved by the people (entrenchment), it should be remembered that no codified constitution can ever be completely comprehensive. For example,

- a codified constitution may be vague, leading to inconsistent interpretation;
- a codified constitution will also be reflective of the time in which it was written, and because of its rigidity be difficult to change.

5. Consequently, in a way similar to uncodified constitutions, the majority of codified constitutions are also supplemented by unwritten standards, rules, practices etc. often to fill any gaps or to allow for adjustment.

6. Finally, the actual effectiveness of a constitution against abuse of power depends on the willingness of the organs of the State to comply with it, the ability of the courts to enforce it and the people to abide by it, regardless of whether it is codified or uncodified.

7. In 2007 the Government published a Green Paper entitled 'The Governance of Britain'. In the conclusion the Paper raised the idea of a written constitution. The Prime Minister, Gordon Brown, also announced the start of national consultations on the issue of creating a British 'Bill of Rights and Responsibilities'. These initiatives may mark the beginnings of the future full codification of the British constitution.

CHAPTER 2

The Sources of Constitutional Law

SOURCES OF THE UK CONSTITUTION

Statute
e.g. Bill of Rights 1688

Common law
e.g. *Entick v Carrington* (1765)

Convention
e.g. appointment of the Prime Minister,
non-legally binding rules

Royal prerogative
e.g. declaring war and/or peace

European Community law
European Communities Act 1972

Other
e.g. parliamentary privilege,
scholarly writings

Since the UK's constitution is uncodified, its sources cannot be found in one, single document. Instead, the UK's constitution is derived from a range of sources, only some of which are written.

2.1 Statute

1. Statute is traditionally considered the primary source of constitutional law in the United Kingdom and is otherwise known as an Act of Parliament. A statute can be amended only by Parliament.

2. There are many examples of constitutionally significant statutes, including the following:
   - **Magna Carta 1215** – a settlement with the Crown, protecting the rights of individuals, freedom of the Church and trial by jury;
   - **Bill of Rights 1688** – altered the balance of power in favour of Parliament over the Crown. After this statute, the Crown required Parliament's consent for certain action, such as raising taxes;
   - **Act of Settlement 1700** – combined with the Bill of Rights to ensure that the monarch could no longer govern by use of the prerogative and marked the point when Parliament became the dominant constitutional organ;
   - **The Treaty of Union 1706** – united England and Scotland under one Parliament.

3. Significant statutes during the last century include, for example:
   - the **Parliament Acts 1911 and 1949** – reducing the power of the House of Lords in the legislative process;
   - the **European Communities Act 1972** – providing for the United Kingdom to become a member of the European Economic Community;
   - the **Scotland, Northern Ireland and Wales Acts 1998** – providing for devolution;

- the **Human Rights Act 1998** – providing for the incorporation of the European Convention on Human Rights; and
- the **Constitutional Reform Act 2005** – providing for, *inter alia*, greater separation of powers (see Chapter 3).

4. Traditionally, all statutes have been considered of equal importance, all being subject to the doctrine of implied repeal, a consequence of parliamentary supremacy (see Chapter 4). There has though been increasing recognition of a **hierarchy** of statutes, witnessed, for example, in the comments of Laws LJ in *Thoburn v Sunderland City Council* (2002).

5. In *Thoburn*, statutes were considered to be of two types: '**ordinary**' statutes and '**constitutional**' statutes. A constitutional statute would be one that would affect the legal relationship between the individual and the State in some general manner, or would enlarge or diminish the scope of fundamental constitutional rights.

6. Laws LJ was of the opinion that the following statutes were examples of constitutional Acts of Parliament:
- Magna Carta 1215;
- Bill of Rights 1688;
- Acts of Union;
- Human Rights Act 1998;
- Scotland Act 1998;
- Government of Wales Act 1998; and
- European Communities Act 1972.

7. Such constitutional statutes are no longer subject to implied repeal because they protect the special status of constitutional rights. Consequently such statutes are subject only to express repeal and are consequently perhaps 'semi-entrenched'. (For further discussion of this in the context of the supremacy of Parliament see Chapter 4. For further discussion of the European Communities Act 1972 see Chapter 8 and for the Human Rights Act 1998 see Chapter 9).

2.2 Common law

1. This source is created by case law, and is also known as **precedent**. Common law is subordinate to statute in that statute on the same subject-matter takes precedence because of the doctrine of parliamentary supremacy. For example, after the decision in *Burmah Oil v Lord Advocate* (1965) Parliament passed the War Damages Act 1965, which overruled the decision of the House of Lords and which, in addition, had retrospective effect. (Parliamentary supremacy is discussed in Chapter 4.)

2. Examples of significant cases that have contributed to the development of constitutional law include:
   - *Prohibitions del Roy* (1607) – where the court concluded that the King was not permitted to act as a judge;
   - *Entick v Carrington* (1765) – where the court concluded that a general warrant for entry into private property and seizure of private property was a trespass and illegal;
   - *Pickin v British Rail Board* (1974) – in which the court held that once an Act of Parliament had passed through the relevant legislative stages, no body could question its validity;
   - *M v Home Office* (1994) – where it was held that the Home Secretary had committed contempt of court by disobeying a judge's order;
   - *R v Secretary of State for Transport, ex parte Factortame (No 2)* (1989) – where it was held that directly enforceable rules of Community law overrode conflicting rules of national law, regardless of their constitutional significance.

3. In addition to generating precedent, the courts also interpret statute where the meaning is disputed. The methods employed to do this are themselves created by judicial decisions and include, for example, the 'literal rule', the 'golden rule' and the 'mischief rule'.

4. Parliament may also impose principles of interpretation on the courts. For example, the Human Rights Act 1998 provides that statute must be interpreted, as far as is possible, so that it conforms to the European Convention on Human Rights (see Chapter 9).

2.3 Constitutional conventions

2.3.1 Definition and examples of conventions

1. A significant number of important constitutional principles are not found in either statute or common law and are unwritten. They are called conventions. Many definitions of conventions can be found including, for example:
   - Austin – the 'positive morality' of the constitution;
   - Mill – the 'unwritten maxims' of the constitution;
   - Freeman – the 'whole system of political morality';
   - Jennings – a source that 'fleshes out the dry bones of the law';
   - Makintosh – 'generally accepted descriptive statements of constitutional and political practice'.
2. Examples of conventions include:
   - the Monarch appoints the Prime Minister but under convention selects the leader of the political party with the majority of seats in the House of Commons;
   - Parliament, according to convention, must meet at least once a year;
   - the Crown has the prerogative to dissolve Parliament but, according to convention, does so on the advice of Ministers.
3. Two of the most important constitutional conventions, designed to secure **executive accountability**, are individual and collective ministerial responsibility. (These conventions are discussed in further detail in Chapter 6.)
4. According to Jennings, the existence of a convention may be determined by asking whether there is precedent for the

rule; whether those operating under the convention believe themselves obligated to do so; and whether there is a reason for the convention.

5. Conventions are therefore **evolutionary** and develop through usage. There is no prescribed time or duration required to establish the existence of a convention. This, combined with their unwritten nature, means that it can be very difficult to identify whether a particular convention exists.

6. However, conventions do offer the constitution **flexibility**. The principles provided in the form of conventions often develop because of a desire to avoid formal change through the production of legislation. Hence conventions can be helpful in easing constitutional change in an informal way, for example:
   - from **monarchy to parliamentary supremacy** – the role of the Monarch in government has effectively disappeared since the 18th century, not as a result of statute, but of conventions. In this way the Prime Minister has also acquired significant government powers;
   - from **Empire to Commonwealth** – the recognition of the right to self-rule for the colonies of the Empire was originally reflected in the use of convention, requiring Westminster to seek the approval of such colonies before it could legislate for them.

2.3.2 The binding nature of conventions

1. The most significant characteristic of conventions is that they are **non-legally binding**.
   - Dicey stated that conventions may regulate conduct but 'are not in reality laws at all since they are not enforced by the courts';
   - Marshall and Moodie describe conventions as 'rules of constitutional behaviour which are considered to be

binding by and upon those who operate the constitution but which are not enforced by the law courts'.

2. However, the courts may recognise the existence of a convention when coming to judgment. For example:

- *Attorney-General v Jonathan Cape Ltd* (1976) – where the court recognised the existence of convention, in this case the convention of collective ministerial responsibility, but would not enforce it *per se* since it was a non-legal rule;

- *Madzimbamuto v Lardner-Burke* (1969) – where it was held that no court could declare an Act of Parliament invalid because it breached a convention, in this case the convention that Westminster seek the approval of colonies before legislating for them;

- *Manuel v Attorney-General* (1983) – where it was confirmed that conventions are non-legal rules and unable to limit parliamentary supremacy. Consequently any Act of Parliament that breaches convention will nevertheless be upheld by the courts.

3. Convention cannot crystallise into law: *Reference Re the Amendment of the Constitution of Canada* (1982). Therefore the only way a convention can become legally binding is if it is put into statutory form. Examples of statutes incorporating former conventions include the Statute of Westminster 1931 and the Parliament Act 1911.

4. The breach of a convention may result in a number of consequences, depending on the importance of the convention itself. Indeed, Dicey stated that the breach of some conventions could result in legal consequences. However, it is rarely the case that breach of a convention will have legal consequences: breaching a convention will most often result in political, not legal, consequences.

5. Therefore, conventions are generally followed not because of legal consequences but because of political difficulties that may arise.

2.3.3 Codifying conventions

There has been much debate on the issue of whether conventions should be codified.

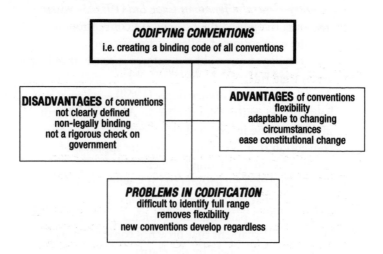

2.4 The Royal Prerogative

1. This source of law derives from common-law powers and is described by Dicey as 'every act which the executive government can lawfully do without the authority of [an] Act of Parliament'. (This source is discussed in further detail in Chapter 6.)
2. There are two main categories of prerogative powers:
   - prerogative powers in relation to foreign affairs,
     - e.g. • power to declare war and peace;
       - power to deploy armed forces abroad;
       - power to make treaties;
   - prerogative powers in relation to domestic affairs,
     - e.g. • power to summon and dissolve Parliament;
       - power to defend the realm;
       - power to grant mercy, pardons and reduce sentences.

3. In constitutional terms the prerogative is an important source because it is not subject to normal legislative procedures, and until the relatively recent landmark judgment in *Council of Civil Service Unions v Minister for the Civil Service* (1985), the exercise of prerogative powers by the executive was not subject to judicial review.

2.5 European Community law

1. The UK Parliament passed the European Communities Act 1972 and thereby agreed to implement and enforce all European Community law.
2. This source of law has become increasingly important, while simultaneously creating difficulties for both the judiciary and politicians.
3. Significant rights have been created by EC law, including those in relation to employment law, sex discrimination, free movement for EC nationals and laws regulating the free movement of goods, services and capital.
4. The primary constitutional significance of EC law is its relationship with UK domestic law, particularly since the UK's constitution operates under the traditional doctrine of parliamentary supremacy. (This is discussed in detail in Chapter 8.)

2.6 Other sources

1. Parliament has sole jurisdiction to determine its own composition and procedure. Thus the law and custom of Parliament (e.g. parliamentary privilege) is a source of constitutional law. (Privilege is discussed in detail in Chapter 5.)
2. The writings of eminent scholars may also be said to be a source of constitutional law, especially since the courts may refer to them. Examples of such scholars include Dicey, Blackstone and Jennings.

CHAPTER 3

Fundamental Constitutional Concepts

THE RULE OF LAW

Means of ensuring the protection of individual rights

DICEY'S PRINCIPLES

1. No person is punishable in body or goods except for a distinct breach of the law	**2.** Every person irrespective of rank is subject to the ordinary law of the land and the jurisdiction of the courts	**3.** Common law creates a system of rights and liberties superior to that offered by any declaration or Bill of Rights

Examples of the doctrine accepted by the courts:
* *Francome v Mirror Group Newspapers* (1984); *Ex parte Bennett* (1994); *M v Home Office* (1994); *A v Secretary of State for the Home Department* (2004)
* Judicial review
* Dicey's principles in the modern constitutional context
* Critique of Dicey's rule of law; modern interpretations

THE SEPARATION OF POWERS

A check and balance system to prevent abuse of power

MONTESQUIEU'S PRINCIPLES

1. Three government functions – legislative, executive and judicial	**2.** Each function should be vested in a separate body	**3.** Each body acts as a check and balance on the others to ensure there is no abuse of power

* Examples: France and the USA
* Extent of the doctrine in the UK: **Fusion** between
  - Legislature and executive
  - Executive and judiciary
  - Judiciary and legislature
  - Personnel
* **Reform**: Constitutional Reform Act 2005

3.1 The rule of law

1. The rule of law is capable of many definitions, based on both philosophical and political theories, and hence it is a difficult doctrine to explain definitively.
2. In basic terms, the rule of law is the supremacy of law over man. As Aristotle explained in the 4th century BC, 'the rule of law is to be preferred to that of any individual'.
3. Carroll defines the rule of law as 'neither a rule nor a law. It is now generally understood as a doctrine of political morality which concentrates on the role of law in securing the correct balance of rights and powers between individuals and the state in free and civilised societies'.
4. The rule of law can be interpreted as:
   - an overarching, universal law that applies to everyone, including the executive and legislature; and
   - that man-made laws should conform to a 'higher' law, the rule of law.
5. The rule of law is consequently often recognised as a means of **ensuring the protection of individual rights against governmental power**.

3.1.1 Dicey and the rule of law

In the United Kingdom, the general concept of the rule of law has become identified with Dicey's explanation of the doctrine in his 1885 text, *The Law of the Constitution*. According to Dicey, the rule of law was a distinct feature of the UK constitution, with three main concepts:

1. No person is punishable in body or goods except for a distinct breach of the law (*Entick v Carrington* (1765)). This concept attempts to ensure that law is not secret, arbitrary or retrospective, thereby limiting the discretionary power of government. To comply with the rule of law, laws should be clear, precise, transparent and accessible.

2. Every person, irrespective of rank, is subject to the ordinary law of the land and the jurisdiction of the courts. Dicey based this principle on the UK system as compared with those of the time in, for example, France, where disputes with government officials were heard in administrative courts separate from the ordinary civil courts and where different rules applied.

3. The common law creates a system of rights and liberties superior to that offered by any declaration or Bill of Rights. This is because the common law system emphasises remedies for infringement of rights rather than merely declaring the content of those rights.

3.1.2 Examples of the rule of law operating in the constitution

1. The existence of administrative law, particularly the process of **judicial review**, enables the courts to ensure power is controlled and the executive is accountable for its actions and is based on the need to ensure the rule of law. (For further discussion of judicial review see Chapters 11 and 12.)

2. Some examples of cases where the courts have referred to the significance of the doctrine in the constitution include:
   - *Francome and Another v Mirror Group Newspapers Ltd and Others* (1984) – where Lord Donaldson referred to the doctrine as one underpinning parliamentary democracy and extending to all citizens;
   - *Merkur Island Shipping Corporation v Laughton and Others* (1983) – where Lord Diplock commented on the need for the law to have clarity;
   - *R v Home Secretary, ex parte Venables* (1988) – the Home Secretary had considered a campaign conducted in a national newspaper when determining the sentencing of convicted children, rather than basing the decision on their progress/rehabilitation in detention. The action was considered 'an abdication of the rule of law';

- *R v Horseferry Road Magistrates' Court, ex parte Bennett* (1994) – where Lord Griffiths noted that it is the responsibility of the courts to maintain the rule of law, to oversee executive action and to not permit action that threatens basic human rights or breaches the rule of law;
- *M v Home Office* (1994) – where, applying Dicey's second proposition that every person is subject to the law, the House of Lords held that the Home Secretary could be found in contempt of court by disobeying an injunction; and
- *A v Secretary of State for the Home Department* (2004) – where the House of Lords held that power to detain indefinitely under the Terrorism, Crime and Security Act 2001 was a breach of both the ECHR and the rule of law.

3.1.3 Dicey's rule of law in the modern constitutional context

If we apply Dicey's concept of the rule of law to the modern constitution, we can make a number of observations:

1. The first concept, that no person may have their body or goods interfered with except for a distinct breach of the law, is in direct contrast to the provisions of some present-day statutes. For example:
   (a) the police have powers of arrest, stop and search when they have only 'reasonable grounds' for suspecting certain facts (see Chapter 10);
   (b) the Government also has power to interfere with a person's goods/property without any breach of the law, for example the exercise of compulsory purchase orders.
2. The second concept formulated by Dicey was that no person is above the law. However, there are a number of contraventions of this principle in the modern constitution. For example:
   (a) the monarch in her personal capacity is not subject to the jurisdiction of the ordinary courts;

(b) the Crown is also in a privileged position in litigation (Crown Proceedings Act 1947) and cannot be sued in tort for the actions of its servants;

(c) no civil action may be brought in respect of the comments or actions of a judge exercising their judicial role (*Anderson v Gorrie* (1895)) or in relation to a jury's verdict (*Bushell's Case* (1670));

(d) Members of Parliament have rights and immunities beyond those granted to the ordinary citizen, such as freedom of expression and freedom from arrest in certain circumstances (see Chapter 5). Conversely, there are individuals who are subject to additional legal restraints. For example, under the Army Act 1955, members of the armed forces are subject to additional legal codes of conduct and offences, such as desertion, and a different judicial system.

3. The third concept, that common law provides protection of individual rights in the UK constitution, remains the case today, although added protection has been provided by virtue of the Human Rights Act 1998 (see Chapter 9).

4. The faith Dicey had in the ability of the common law to protect rights and liberties, though, has been criticised.

(a) Dicey failed to appreciate that the effectiveness of the common law in offering such protection can be reduced by the pre-eminence given to statute, a consequence of the supremacy of Parliament (see Chapter 4).

(b) Hence, while the common law may offer protection in the form of remedies for those whose rights are infringed, statute may remove that protection, as was the case in *Burmah Oil v Lord Advocate* (1965).

3.1.4 Critique of Dicey's rule of law

1. Sir Ivor Jennings claimed that Dicey's standard of the rule of law was influenced by his political views and that the phrase could be used to describe any society where a state of law and order exists.

2. Consequently, the rule of law is seen to operate 'best' in societies that meet Dicey's standards. Jennings instead claimed that the rule of law may exist in societies that do not meet Dicey's standards – in other words, that the rule of law can exist in political systems other than those based on traditional Western democratic models.

3. Modern interpretations of the rule of law include:

   (i) **the rule of law as a political concept**

   Laws should exhibit particular characteristics and meet minimum standards in terms of the way they are expressed and administered. For example, Raz argues that the making of laws should be guided by the following principles:

   - Laws should be **general** (i.e. not discriminate), **prospective**, **open** and **clear**;
   - Laws should be relatively **stable** (i.e. should not be subject to frequent and unnecessary amendment);
   - **Making delegated legislation** should be guided by **clear, stable, open general rules**;
   - There should be a guaranteed **independent judiciary**;
   - The application of law should accord with the rules of **natural justice** (i.e. there should be no bias and there should be the right to a fair hearing);
   - The courts must have the power to **review** law-making and administrative action to ensure it is compliant with these rules;
   - The courts should be **easily accessible** (i.e. access to justice should not be hindered by excessive delays and expense); and
   - The **discretion of crime preventing bodies** should not be allowed to pervert the law (i.e. agencies such as the police should not be able to choose which laws to enforce and when).

   However, this approach has been criticised as placing too much emphasis on procedure as a means of protecting rights, whilst failing to actually identify the nature and extent of the rights themselves.

(ii) **the rule of law as a substantive concept**

Laws should not be morally neutral. Dworkin, for example, argues that laws should contain fundamental values i.e. be 'morally good'. However, this interpretation is not universally agreed with because many 'values' are not capable of concrete definition, for example the right to life versus abortion and hunting versus animal welfare.

(iii) **The Declaration of Delhi 1959**

This was issued by the International Commission of Jurists and declares that the purpose of all law should be respect for the 'supreme value of human personality'. The Declaration identified that a constitution observing the Rule of Law would have:

- **Representative government** – in the UK we have free and fair elections but there are concerns as to whether the electoral system is capable of providing a truly representative government (see Chapter 5).
- **Respect for basic human rights** – this has been enhanced with the passing of the Human Rights Act 1998 (see Chapter 9).
- **No retrospective penal laws** – judicial practice is not to accept retrospective legislation generally, unless an Act expressly permits such application in which case the courts must abide by it because of parliamentary supremacy. However, such laws would probably breach both the ECHR and EC law.
- **Ability to bring proceedings against the State** – provided by, for example, judicial review (see Chapters 11 and 12).
- **Right to a fair trial** including the presumption of innocence, legal representation, bail and the right to appeal – these characteristics apply in the English legal system, although there are criticisms of the reduction in legal aid impacting on the ability for many to pursue legal action;

- **Independent judiciary** – applicable to the English legal system and now enhanced with the passing of the Constitutional Reform Act 2005 (see 3.2.5).
- **Adequate control of delegated legislation** – there are criticisms of the ability of the executive to pass delegated legislation without sufficient checks and balances.

3.2 The separation of powers

1. This ancient doctrine, which can be traced back to Aristotle, was perhaps most thoroughly explained by the French jurist, Montesquieu, who based his analysis on the British constitution of the early 18th century.
2. The doctrine is based on the notion that there are three distinct functions of government – **legislative**, **executive** and **judicial** functions. According to the doctrine in its basic form, these three functions should be vested in distinct bodies so that excessive power is not concentrated in the hands of one body. To do otherwise could lead to abuse of power or what Montesquieu termed 'tyranny'.
3. This concept of the doctrine has, however, been re-interpreted by, for example, Blackstone, to mean that it is not necessary for distinct bodies to hold each power, with no influence over each other, but that what is required is a '**check and balance**' system operating between them – sometimes referred to as the theory of 'mixed government'.

3.2.1 Examples of the separation of powers doctrine

Different constitutions have adopted different approaches to applying the separation of powers.

1. In France there is not complete separation of powers but the doctrine can be witnessed, for example, in the judiciary's inability to question the validity or interfere

with the functions of the legislature.

2. In the United States of America a 'check and balance' system operates under the 1787 constitution.

- Consequently, the legislature (Congress, comprising the House of Representatives and the Senate), executive (President) and judiciary (federal courts and Supreme Court) operate in a 'creative tension' whereby each can check the other.
- For example, the Supreme Court can declare legislation unconstitutional; the President is elected separately from Congress and neither they nor their Cabinet can sit or vote in Congress; and Congress (the Senate) must approve presidential nominations for executive office.

3.2.2 The extent of the doctrine in the modern British constitution

1. The three organs of government do exist in the modern British constitution and to a certain extent there is separation of powers (e.g. judicial independence and judicial refusal to intervene in legislative and executive matters such as parliamentary privilege).

2. The courts have confirmed that the British constitution features the doctrine. For example:

- In *R v Secretary of State for the Home Department, ex parte Fire Brigades Union and Others* (1995) Lord Mustill spoke of Parliament, the executive and the courts each having 'their distinct and largely exclusive domain'.
- In *Duport Steels Ltd v Sirs* (1980) Lord Denning stated that the British constitution was 'firmly based' on the doctrine, with the result that 'Parliament makes the laws, the judiciary interprets them'.
- In *R v HM Treasury, ex parte Smedley* (1985) Sir John Donaldson MR stated 'it is a constitutional convention of the highest importance that the legislature and the judicature are separate and independent of one another'.

3. There is also some separation in terms of personnel. For example, the majority of positions within the executive, such as civil servants and members of the armed forces, disqualify the holder from membership of the legislature (House of Commons Disqualification Act 1975). To some extent, each body also acts as a check on the other (e.g. judicial review, see Chapters 11 and 12).

4. However, there is also considerable overlap of functions and personnel, sometimes described as 'fusion', and ultimately the 'check and balance' system is subject to the principle that Parliament is sovereign.

3.2.3 Examples of fusion in the British constitution

The legislature and executive

1. The result of the British electoral system combined with the party system produces a dominant executive that actually sits within the legislature (by convention, positions within the executive can be held only by Members of either House of Parliament).

2. This executive, through strict Party discipline and powers to control debate within the House of Commons, is capable of effectively depriving the legislature of its true function.

3. The legislature has delegated power to Ministers so that they may deal with issues through the production of statutory instruments (delegated legislation), although this is subject to some parliamentary scrutiny.

4. Ministers also have residual prerogative powers, which result in the ability to legislate without the consent of Parliament (Orders in Council). This power is to some limited extent 'checked' by the courts under the process of judicial review (see Chapters 11 and 12).

The executive and judiciary

1. Members of the judiciary are appointed by the executive.

2. The creation of numerous tribunals under statute has resulted in executive/administrative bodies hearing disputes between private individuals and between private individuals and government departments.

3. There are also disputes between private individuals and executive authority that may be determined only by a Minister, in other words, a member of the executive. For example, this is the case in relation to planning permission by a local authority and challenging compulsory purchase orders. This offers a clear example of the executive performing a judicial function.

The judiciary and the legislature

1. Unlike those systems with a codified constitution, there is no provision within the British constitution for a court to challenge primary legislation and declare it unconstitutional. Consequently, there is no ultimate check on the legislature from the judiciary. However, in the case of delegated legislation the judiciary can employ judicial review: see *R v HM Treasury, ex parte Smedley* (1985). See Chapters 11 and 12.

2. The judiciary is to some extent capable of creating law, which should, under the doctrine, be a role reserved for the legislature. This occurs through the process of precedent, creating common law. This was described in *Shaw v DPP* (1962), in the context of criminal law, as a 'residual power to enforce the supreme and fundamental purpose of the law'.

3. The House of Lords also performs a fused role, being both the superior court of law in the English legal system and the second chamber of the bicameral legislature. Note changes introduced by the Constitutional Reform Act 2005 at 3.2.5.

Fusion of personnel

1. The Prime Minister is head of the Cabinet and therefore the executive, yet under convention must be a Member of

Parliament, elected to the House of Commons.

2. Ministers are members of the Cabinet (the executive) and usually also Members of Parliament (the legislature).

3. Judges sitting in the House of Lords in its capacity as the highest court in the English legal system are also members of the House of Lords as the upper chamber of the legislature. However, under convention they do not participate in purely political debates. (Note changes introduced by the Constitutional Reform Act 2005 at 3.2.5 below.)

3.2.4 A modern analysis of the separation of powers

1. There have been a number of more modern examinations of the doctrine and its application to the British constitution. Marshall argues that the doctrine lacks any significant definition and is inconsistent. Professor Wade claims that the British constitution exhibits only one example of the doctrine, namely judicial independence.

2. However, the judiciary has repeatedly asserted the existence of the doctrine in the British constitution (see 3.2.2). Professor Munro therefore concludes that whilst the doctrine is 'rooted in constitutional tradition', it is neither 'absolute nor a predominant feature of the British constitution'.

3.2.5 Recent reform

1. The statements above, however, now need to be read in light of the **Constitutional Reform Act 2005**. The Act provides for moves towards a more formal separation of executive, legislative and judicial powers and a removal of some of the fusion that has been created as a result of historical anomalies.

2. The key reforms include the following:
   a) **Judicial independence**

- For the first time the Act enshrines in law a duty on government ministers to uphold the independence of the judiciary. They are specifically barred from trying to influence judicial decisions through any special access to judges.
- This should aid in ensuring that the rule of law is upheld (see 3.1).

b) A Supreme Court of the United Kingdom

- A major innovation of the Act was to introduce the idea of a new Supreme Court, replacing the Appellate Committee of the House of Lords, thus separating the highest court from Parliament, the legislature.
- The jurisdiction of the Supreme Court is that of the Appellate Committee, as well as the jurisdiction of the Judicial Committee of the Privy Council in respect of devolution matters.
- All existing Law Lords will become justices of the court, but they will remain full members of the House of Lords.
- The new court has its own building (the previous Middlesex Guildhall Crown Court) and is scheduled to open in October 2009.

c) Judicial Appointments Commission

- The Act establishes an independent Judicial Appointments Commission, responsible for selecting candidates to recommend for judicial appointment to the Secretary of State for Constitutional Affairs.
- Appointments are thus still based on the criterion of merit but within a process that is more modern, open and transparent.

d) Reforming the role of the Lord Chancellor

- The office of the Lord Chancellor was considered one of the most glaring examples of the fusion of powers within the constitution. Traditionally the Lord Chancellor was a member of the executive and sat in the Cabinet. As head of the judiciary the Lord Chancellor presided over the House of Lords when exercising its judicial function. As a member of the House of Lords the position also offered membership of the legislature.

- The original Constitutional Reform Bill proposed abolition of the role of Lord Chancellor but this was rejected by the House of Lords. Instead the Act modified the role, now known as the Secretary of State for Constitutional Affairs.

- In particular, the judicial functions of the Lord Chancellor were transferred to the Lord Chief Justice. The Lord Chief Justice is responsible for the training, guidance and deployment of judges and represents the views of the judiciary to Parliament and Ministers.

- The Lord Chancellor was also replaced as the Speaker of the House of Lords by the Lord Speaker.

Powers of the Lord Chancellor before and after the Constitutional Reform Act 2005		
Powers/ function	Pre CRA 2005	Post CRA 2005
Legislative powers/ functions	Speaker of the House of Lords	Replaced by the Lord Speaker
Executive powers/ functions	Member of the Cabinet	Member of the Cabinet
Judicial powers/ functions	Head of the judiciary	Replaced by the Lord Chief Justice
	Appointed judges	Replaced by Judicial Appointments Commission

CHAPTER 4

The Supremacy of Parliament

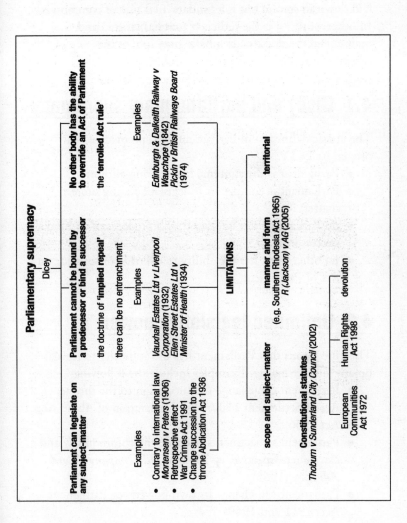

One of the key characteristics of the British constitution is the dominance of the legislature, Parliament. A result of the historical struggle between the Crown and Parliament (culminating in the Bill of Rights 1688), the doctrine is not laid down in statute but is a fundamental rule of common law. In other words, it is the judiciary that has created and maintained the doctrine as a basic principle of the constitution.

4.1 Dicey and parliamentary supremacy

The classic definition of parliamentary supremacy is that offered by Dicey:
- Parliament is the supreme law-making authority;
- Parliament is competent to legislate on any subject-matter;
- no Parliament can be bound by a predecessor or bind a successor;
- no other body has the ability to override or set aside an Act of Parliament.

4.2 Unlimited legislative power

This rule means that Parliament has the authority to legislate on any subject-matter. Examples include the following:
- Parliament can change the succession to the throne, eg Act of Settlement 1700; HM Declaration of Abdication Act 1936.
- Parliament's enactments override the common law and can be retrospective, eg *Burmah Oil Company v Lord Advocate* (1965).
- Parliament can change its own powers, eg Parliament Acts 1911 and 1949.
- Parliament can grant independence to dependent states, eg Nigeria Independence Act 1960; Zimbabwe Independence Act 1979.

- Parliament can legislate with retrospective effect, eg War Damage Act 1965; War Crimes Act 1991.
- Parliament can legislate contrary to international law, eg *Mortensen v Peters* (1906); *Cheney v Conn* (1968).

Note:
Only an Act of Parliament is 'supreme'. Resolutions of either House do not have the force of law unless put on a statutory basis (*Stockdale v Hansard* (1839)); proclamations of the Crown issued under the prerogative do not have the force of law; and treaties, also entered into under the prerogative, cannot have the force of law, unless incorporated by statute.

4.3 No Parliament can be bound by a predecessor or bind a successor

1. Each and every Parliament must be supreme in its own right. Consequently, no Parliament can be bound by a preceding Parliament, or bind a future one. The mechanism for securing this principle is known as the **doctrine of implied repeal**.

2. Parliament may expressly repeal any previous law. The courts must then give effect to the later statute. However, Parliament may not expressly repeal earlier legislation leaving two or more conflicting statutes. The doctrine of implied repeal then applies, in that the courts are required to apply the latest statute, considering earlier law to be impliedly repealed – see *Vauxhall Estates Ltd v Liverpool Corporation* (1932) and *Ellen Street Estates Ltd v Minister of Health* (1934).

3. The consequence of the application of implied repeal is that no legislation can be entrenched, in other words protected from future changes in the law that Parliament may wish to make.

4.4 No other body has the ability to override or set aside an Act of Parliament

1. Before the Bill of Rights 1688, it was not uncommon for the courts to declare an Act of Parliament invalid because it did not conform to a higher, divine law or the law of nature (*Dr Bonham's Case* (1610) and *Day v Savadge* (1615)).

2. The courts no longer assert this authority and instead apply the principle that once an Act is passed, it is the law. This is known as the **enrolled Act rule**. Consequently, the enforcement of the procedural rules for creating an Act is in the hands of Parliament and the courts will refuse to consider whether there have been any procedural defects – see *Edinburgh and Dalkeith Railway v Wauchope* (1842), *Lee v Bude and Torrington Junction Railway Co.* (1871) and *Pickin v British Railways Board* (1974). All a court can do therefore is to construe and apply Acts of Parliament.

Note:

In order for an Act to exist, it must comply with the requirements of common law. A Bill becomes an Act if it has been approved by both Houses of Parliament (unless the Parliament Acts 1911 and 1949 are invoked) and has received the Royal Assent. Other requirements, such as standing orders, conventions and practices govern the passage of a Bill through the Houses and the enforcement of these rules is a matter entirely for Parliament.

4.5 Limitations to parliamentary supremacy

Whilst it appears that Parliament can legislate on anything it wishes, that no legislation can be entrenched and therefore protected from future change, and that no other body can question the validity of a statute, there are significant limitations imposed on Parliament's supremacy.

Limitations as to manner and form

1. An example of this can be seen in the Colonial Laws Validity Act 1865 and its interpretation in *Attorney-General for New South Wales v Trethowan* (1932). In this case the New South Wales legislature was bound in the way in which it abolished its Upper House.

2. However, this precedent is a weak one when applied to the question of whether the British Parliament can limit itself as to the manner and form of subsequent legislation; the New South Wales legislature was different to the British Parliament in that it was a subordinate legislature, consequently bound to follow the law prescribed by Westminster.

3. In *R (Jackson) v Attorney-General* (2005) it was argued that the Parliament Act 1949 was invalid and that consequently the Hunting Act 2004 passed under it was also invalid. The House of Lords held that the 1949 Act was valid. Consequently it appears that the Parliament Acts could technically be used to achieve constitutional change without the consent of the House of Lords.

4. However, this was expressly doubted by Lord Steyn, who implied that the courts would have a role in ascertaining whether the Acts' use was constitutionally proper or correct. Using the Acts in such a way would probably also raise considerable political criticism.

Territorial limitations

1. Whilst Parliament may technically have the authority to legislate for anywhere in the world (extra-territorial jurisdiction), there are geographical limitations to the ability to enforce that law. Hence, the practical consequences render the law unenforceable and therefore redundant.

2. For example, in 1965 Parliament attempted to assert control over what was then Southern Rhodesia by passing the Southern Rhodesia Act. This invalidated any legislation passed in the country. Parliament's competence to pass such an Act was affirmed in *Madzimbamuto v Lardner-Burke* (1969). However, the practical effectiveness of the Act was limited by the fact that it could not be enforced. Hence, *de jure* power may have rested in the Westminster Parliament, but *de facto* power was in the hands of the Rhodesian Government.

3. We can see this recognised by the courts.
- In *Blackburn v Attorney-General* (1971) Lord Denning acknowledged that legal theory (parliamentary supremacy) had to sometimes give way to 'practical politics'. An example would be Parliament trying to reverse grants of independence.
- Similarly, in *Manuel and Others v Attorney-General* (1983) Megarry VC noted that 'legal validity is one thing, enforceability is another'.

Limitations as to scope and subject matter

1. In *Thoburn v Sunderland City Council* (2002) a hierarchy of statutes was recognised. **Constitutional statutes** were considered as not subject to implied repeal because they protect the special status of constitutional rights. Hence such Acts are to some extent entrenched and limit parliamentary supremacy in the context of what it may legislate on.

2. Examples of such statutes include:
- Magna Carta 1215;
- Bill of Rights 1688;
- Acts of Union; and
- Reform Acts.

3. However the most significant of these constitutional statutes are:

a) European Communities Act 1972

- The European Communities Act 1972 section 2(4) requires that all past and future legislation be compatible with EC law. This has become a significant limitation on parliamentary supremacy and is discussed in detail in Chapter 8.

b) The Human Rights Act 1998

- In the context of this Act, implied repeal is effectively removed because if Parliament wishes to legislate contrary to the provisions of the ECHR it can only do so expressly. This is the effect of the duty of interpretation imposed on the courts under section 3 of the Act.
- Clarification of Parliament's intentions in terms of complying with human rights can be seen in any statements of compatibility issued under section 19. (The Act is discussed in detail in Chapter 9.)

c) Devolution

- In *Thoburn* (above) the Acts providing for devolution were specifically cited as examples of constitutional statutes not subject to implied repeal.

Scotland

- The Scotland Act 1998 established a Scottish Parliament, which has the power to make statutes within the sphere of competence laid down in the Act. Section 29 provides that any Act made outside of this legislative competence will not be considered as law.
- The legislative competence of the Scottish Parliament does not affect the power of the Westminster Parliament to still make laws for Scotland, which is a reflection of its continued supremacy: s 28.

- In addition certain matters are reserved to the Westminster Parliament. These are:
  - the constitution;
  - the registration of political parties;
  - foreign affairs;
  - the Civil Service; and
  - defence and treason.
- There are additional, 'reserved' matters, which mean that in such areas the Westminster Parliament can retain uniformity across the UK, whilst devolving power to the Scottish Parliament to deal with the matter as it thinks fit. These include, *inter alia*:
  - financial and economic matters;
  - home affairs;
  - trade and industry;
  - energy;
  - transport, social security, regulation of the professions;
  - employment;
  - health and medicines; and
  - media and culture.
- The Scottish Parliament has the power to increase or decrease the basic rate of income tax set by the Westminster Parliament by a maximum amount of three pence in the pound.

Wales

- The Government of Wales Act 1998 devolved powers to a directly-elected Welsh Assembly, which assumed responsibilities formerly exercised by the Secretary of State for Wales.
- Under the Act the Assembly had law-making powers that were restricted to secondary legislation.
- The Government of Wales Act 2006 conferred additional legislative power. It identifies matters on

which the Assembly may legislate; legislation on
matters outside of this competence is not
considered law.

- The 2006 Act also preserves the right of the
  Westminster Parliament to legislate for Wales: s 93.
- Assembly Measures (subordinate legislation) can be
  passed on a range of 20 different competencies.
  They cannot be used to amend various Acts
  including the European Communities Act 1972
  and the Human Rights Act 1998.
- Assembly Acts (primary legislation) can be passed
  but only if a referendum is held and the outcome
  approves the passing of the Act: Government of
  Wales Act 2006, s 105.

Northern Ireland

- The Northern Ireland Act 1998 provides for the
  Northern Ireland Assembly and a power-sharing
  executive.
- The Assembly can legislate in the form of Acts of
  the Assembly: s 5 Northern Ireland Act 1998. The
  legislative competence of the Assembly is identified
  and, as in the cases of both Scotland and Wales,
  legislation outside of this competence is not to be
  considered law: ss 6 and 7.

4. However, it should be noted that all of the above
   limitations, which can come only in the form of statute,
   could be argued to be self-imposed; no other body can
   place such obligations on Parliament except itself. In theory
   at least, therefore, Parliament may repeal such legislation,
   although it would have to do so expressly. Such action, in
   reality, is highly unlikely in the above contexts.

CHAPTER 5

Parliament

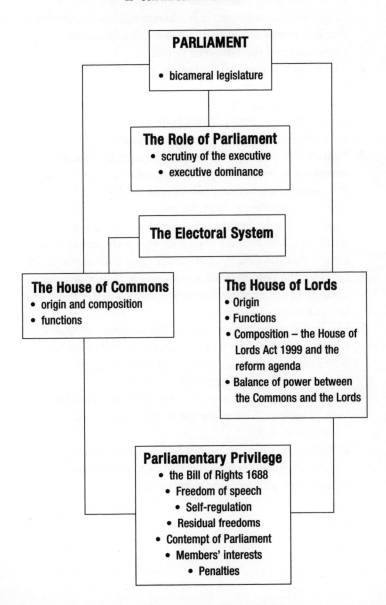

PARLIAMENT
- bicameral legislature

The Role of Parliament
- scrutiny of the executive
- executive dominance

The Electoral System

The House of Commons
- origin and composition
- functions

The House of Lords
- Origin
- Functions
- Composition – the House of Lords Act 1999 and the reform agenda
- Balance of power between the Commons and the Lords

Parliamentary Privilege
- the Bill of Rights 1688
- Freedom of speech
- Self-regulation
- Residual freedoms
- Contempt of Parliament
- Members' interests
- Penalties

5.1 Parliament

1. Parliament is the main legislative body in the United Kingdom's constitution. It is a **bicameral** body, meaning that it is comprised of two chambers, the House of Commons and the House of Lords.

2. The main functions of Parliament are:
   - to sustain the executive by authorising the raising and spending of funds;
   - to hold the executive to account; and
   - to scrutinise, approve or amend legislation.

3. Perhaps the most significant of these roles is to secure **executive accountability** and Parliament attempts to do this using a range of methods. These are discussed at 6.3.

4. Parliament's ability to hold the executive accountable is weakened by the fact that the executive has become dominant. The primary reason for this is the strong party system that has developed since the early 20th century. The first past the post electoral system (see 5.2) supports the creation of a strong, two-party system and makes it difficult for smaller parties to win seats.

5. The ability of Parliament to hold the executive accountable is impacted on by the party system in the following ways:
   - the electoral system can result in the party holding executive power having a large majority;
   - control of parliamentary business and the timetable in the House of Commons rest largely in the hands of the executive; and
   - Parliament exercises its will by voting but each party has a 'whip' system, which is designed to enforce party discipline and persuade members to vote in a certain way.

5.2 Elections

5.2.1 The electoral system

1. The principle of universal adult suffrage was not fully realised in the UK until the 1920s, and is based upon one equal vote per voter. The rules for eligibility of voters are contained in the Representation of the People Act 1983. A voter must be an adult, a citizen of the UK (or an EU citizen for local elections), and registered on the electoral roll of a local authority.

   Certain factors will disqualify an individual from voting:
   - being a minor;
   - being subject to a Mental Health Act incapacity;
   - being in prison;
   - being a peer of the realm;
   - being convicted of an electoral offence; and
   - being an alien.

2. Eligibility for standing as a candidate in an election is governed by the House of Commons Disqualification Act 1975. The following categories are disqualified:
   - holders of judicial office;
   - civil servants;
   - police officers and members of the armed forces; and
   - Crown appointees.

   There are also restrictions upon individual eligibility:
   - the minimum age is 21;
   - no one may stand who has a mental incapacity;
   - peers may not stand unless they renounce their title;
   - clergymen may not stand while they remain in office;
   - bankrupts may not stand until discharged;
   - persons convicted of treason may not stand until rehabilitated; and
   - persons convicted of electoral offences are banned for a period of years.

3. The voting system in the United Kingdom was traditionally a simple majority system known as **'first past the post'** or 'plurality' system. In such a system a winning candidate need achieve only one more vote than the next candidate in a constituency in order to take a seat as a Member of Parliament (MP).

4. Criticisms of the first past the post system include the fact that it is defective in securing democratic representation since it ignores all votes except for the winning candidate. Hence the smaller political parties and minorities often have little or no representation. For example, in 1951 Labour won more votes than the Conservatives but lost the election; in 1974 the Conservatives won more votes than Labour but lost the election; in 1983 the Liberal Party gained 25% of the votes but won only 3.5% of the seats; and in 2001 Labour won only 40.7% of votes but secured 62.6% of seats in the House of Commons.

5. In 2005 the General Election results were as follows:

2005 General Election (First Past the Post)			
Party	**% votes cast**	**% of seats**	**No. of seats**
Labour	35.2	54.9	355
Conservative	32.4	30.7	198
Lib Dem	22.0	9.6	62
Other	10.4	4.8	31

Labour won only 35.2% of total votes cast (9.6 million votes). This was the lowest ever share of votes recorded for a winning party (5.5% lower than 2001). It was equivalent to only 21.6% of the electorate.

6. Recent changes have introduced forms of proportional representation to elect certain representatives and moved the United Kingdom to a position where there is a **'mixed'** electoral system (see table below). The first past the post system is, however, still used to elect Members of Parliament.

Types of proportional representation system	Used to elect
Party List System	**Members of the European Parliament** (MEP)
Additional Member System	**Members of the Scottish Parliament** (Scotland Act 1998) **Members of the Welsh Assembly** (Wales Act 1998) **Members of the London Assembly** (Greater London Authority Act 1999)

5.2.2 Constituencies

1. The UK is divided into 659 constituencies, each represented by one Member of Parliament (MP). Each constituency should be approximately the same in terms of voter numbers and distribution and the boundaries should respect local government boundaries. However, in practice there can be considerable differences between constituencies in terms of both geographical size and voting population.
2. The review of boundaries is now the responsibility of the Boundary Committees. The criteria for review of boundaries allow discretion in their exercise (*R v Boundary Commission for England, ex parte Foot* (1983), *R v Home Secretary, ex parte McWhirter* (1969) and *Harper v Secretary of State for the Home Department* (1955)).

5.2.3 The Political Parties Elections and Referendums Act 2000

The PPERA introduced new controls on party spending and campaign funding and established the Electoral Commission with wide responsibilities for the conduct of elections. The Act regulates the activities of a range of participants.

Object	Definition	Control	Offence
Political parties	Any party wishing to field candidates in any election	Obligation to register party details centrally and lodge the party constitution and accounts	Failure to register details will mean party cannot stand
Third parties	A person or body wishing to promote a party and donate funds	Registration allows much higher spending limit than if not registered	Spending above prescribed limit
Permitted participants	A person or body wishing to promote a particular referendum result	Similar to those for third parties	As above
Donors	Donations to political causes	Must report if total more than £5,000 to a party or £1,000 to an individual	Failure to report
Recipients	Responsibility of party officer	Within 30 days of accepting, must report	Failure to report (weekly at election time) large donations (as above)

Commission of an offence renders the offender ineligible to participate in future elections.

5.2.4 Expenditure

1. For the first time under the PPERA there is a limit on party campaign spending at a national level.
2. It is an offence to exceed the limits, which are set by reference to the number of candidates fielded by the party and the type of election: national or regional. The limits do not apply to local government elections but they do include benefits in kind.
3. Expenditure in constituencies by individual candidates is controlled by the Representation of the People Act 1983.

4. Each candidate must make returns on expenditure via an agent and it is an offence (unauthorised expenditure) to exceed the limits set from time to time (see *R v Tronoh Mines Ltd* (1952)).

5. Expenditure may also be unauthorised, according to *DPP v Luft* (1983), if the campaign does not actually promote a particular candidate, but campaigns against them.

6. According to *Walker v Unison* (1995) a general attack (in this case by advertisement) on a political party does not contravene the Representation of the People Act 1983.

5.2.5 The Electoral Commission

1. The Electoral Commission was established as a new independent body charged with responsibility for all aspects of elections, local and general or regional, in the UK. It comprises:
   - the Chairman;
   - five Commissioners;
   - the Chief Executive.

   The body as a whole is accountable to Parliament.

2. Its statutory duties are:
   - reporting on the administration of elections;
   - reviewing law and practice;
   - promoting awareness of issues and systems to the public; and
   - compiling an annual report.

3. The Commission deals with, for example:
   - registrations of donations received;
   - monitoring of bans on foreign donations;
   - control of campaign expenditure;
   - maintenance of various registers;
   - monitoring of compliance with the PPERA.

4. The Commission keeps the future development of electoral systems and regulations under review and produces consultative documents to invite debate, comment and new ideas, such as the expansion of electronic voting systems and consideration of associated security concerns.

5.2.6 Broadcasting

1. Under the Broadcasting Act 1980, the ITC has limited regulations and duties. Within a requirement to be impartial, it, and the BBC under its Charter, have some editorial control over the exact allocation of airtime to each party. This is based upon the level of support at the last General Election. New parties will therefore not receive much, if any, airtime.
2. Legal challenges to the allocation of broadcast time have not generally been successful (*R v British Broadcasting Corporation, ex parte Referendum Party* (1997)).
3. However, the court found that there had been unlawful action in basing allocation on seats won rather than votes cast in *R v Broadcasting Complaints Commission, ex parte Owen* (1985) but the broad allocation between the leading three parties remained the same.
4. In *R (Pro-Life Alliance) v BBC* (2003) the House of Lords concluded that the BBC and other broadcasters had the right to refuse to show Party political broadcasts on the basis that they would be offensive.

5.3 The House of Commons

5.3.1 Origins and composition

1. The House of Commons was established by the 13th century but was recognisable as the representative body we see today only in the 19th century, following a programme of reforms of electoral practices.
2. There are 659 elected MPs in total, allied to the Government, the Opposition parties or an independent party. Each Member represents a constituency in the House.
3. Under the Parliament Act 1949, the maximum length of a Parliament is five years but it is the prerogative of the Prime Minister to set the exact date for a General Election

and to ask the monarch to dissolve Parliament.

4. The Prime Minister and the Cabinet sit on the front bench facing the leader of the Opposition and the Shadow Cabinet. The rest of the Members sit on the benches behind and it is these backbenchers who are needed to vote in support of a Bill.

5.3.2 The functions of the House of Commons

1. The main functions of the House are as follows:

a Indirect choosing of the government by virtue of the convention that the political party that commands a majority in the House is entitled to form the government;

b Approval of taxation and expenditure;

c Scrutiny and approval of legislation; Bills introduced in Parliament undergo the following procedure:

First Reading	A formal introduction without debate
Second Reading	Substantive debate
Committee Stage	Detailed scrutiny
Third Reading	Amendments approved or rejected
Division	House of Commons votes (legislation then proceeds to the House of Lords, unless it was introduced there, and then presented for the Royal Assent)

d Supervising of the executive occurs in the House of Commons since by convention Ministers are accountable to Parliament. The House of Commons can require a government to resign by a vote of no confidence;

e The redress of grievances raised by an MP on behalf of their constituents; and

f Debating matters of public concern, such as the Iraq War, although it should be noted that there are limited procedural opportunities for such debates.

5.4 The House of Lords

5.4.1 Origins

1. The House of Lords is the oldest part of Parliament and derives from the circle of advisers to the monarch who were rewarded with lands and titles. A hereditary peerage passes from generation to generation, usually through the male line, and, until recently, entitled the holder to sit in the Lords as of right. There were more than 750 hereditary peers in the Lords.

2. The Life Peerages Act 1958 gave non-hereditary peers the right to a seat in the Lords, usually after a period of service in the Commons, or as recognition of their contribution to society.

5.4.2 The functions of the House of Lords

1. The main function of a second chamber in a bicameral legislative body is to act as a revising chamber to scrutinise legislation proposed by the first chamber ensuring that there is a constitutional safeguard.

2. According to the Wakeham Commission 2000, the functions of the House of Lords included the following:

   a to provide advice on public policy and a forum for general debate on matters of public concern without party political pressures;

   b to act as a revising chamber scrutinising the details of proposed legislation;

   c to introduce relatively uncontroversial legislation or private bills as a means of reducing the workload of the House of Commons;

   d to provide Ministers;

   e to provide Committees to discuss general topics e.g. European Communities Committee;

   f to permit persons other than politicians to participate in government (Life Peerages Act 1958);

   g to act as a 'constitutional watchdog'; and

h to act as the highest judicial appellate body in the United Kingdom (note the change that will be introduced by the Constitutional Reform Act 2005: see Chapter 3 for more detail).

3. However, the ability of the House of Lords to carry out these functions was always undermined by criticism of its unrepresentative and undemocratic composition.

5.4.3   Composition before 1999

1. In addition to hereditary and life peers, the Lords included the Lords Spiritual, namely the bishops and archbishops of the Church of England, and the Lords of Appeal in Ordinary, who sit as an Appellate Committee and who are specialist judges.
2. The composition of the Lords attracted much comment and criticism, principally directed towards the undemocratic nature of the hereditary peers' right to sit in the House.
3. Throughout the 20th century, reforms and abolition proposals were made but none were implemented until the Labour Government of 1997 came to power with a specific reform agenda, which according to its manifesto was to replace the House with an elected second chamber using proportional representation.

5.4.4 The House of Lords Act 1999 and the reform agenda

1. The House of Lords Act 1999 removed the voting rights of hereditary peers and members of the Royal Family, although prior to the enactment of the Act a deal was struck between the Government and the Leader of the Lords concerned for the continuity of the House in the interim period before the reforms were completed. As a consequence, 92 peers were selected to continue to serve until the final shape of the House was established.
2. A Royal Commission was established to consider the process of further reform and to make recommendations.

It produced a report in 2000 (the Wakeham Report) recommending a House of 550 members, with the majority being nominated and the rest being selected or elected to represent regional interests. There was no agreement on the number of selected or elected members or their method of selection, but three models were suggested:

- **Model A** = 65 members selected by dividing up the regional allocation of seats according to each Party's share of the vote in that region in the General Election and one third of the regions selecting regional members at each General Election;
- **Model B** = 87 members elected directly using proportional representation at the same time as the European Parliament elections;
- **Model C** = 195 regional members elected at the same time as the European Parliament elections.

The Report also recommended that the system of granting honours should not result in membership of the House and that nominations for the House be by an independent commission.

3. In 2000 the House of Lords Appointments Commission was established. It makes recommendations for non-party political peerages and vets all nominations from political parties.

4. In 2001 the Government produced a White Paper on further reform of the House with the aim of reducing the number of members from 700 to 600 over ten years: 120 would be directly elected; 322 nominated by party leaders; 120 chosen by the Appointments Commission; and the number of bishops reduced to 16 from 26. In 2003 the House of Commons rejected all options for reform and the Lords voted for a fully-appointed House.

5. In 2007 the Government produced a new White Paper proposing a membership of 540 with 20% non-party and 30% appointed party political representation. Elections would be by the 'partially open list system' at the same

time as European Parliament elections; appointment would be by the Appointments Commission.

6. The Constitutional Reform Act 2005 also contained reform of the House in terms of its functions. It provided for the removal of the judicial function of the House and the creation of a new, independent Supreme Court (see Chapter 3 for further detail).

5.4.5 The balance of power between the House of Commons and the House of Lords

1. Prior to the Parliament Act 1911, the House of Lords had equal power with the House of Commons except for financial measures. According to convention, the Lords recognised the supremacy of the Commons in this respect.

2. This convention was breached in 1909. The resulting political conflict preceded the passing of the Parliament Act 1911, which left the Lords with the power to delay Money Bills for one month and non-Money Bills for two years. The power of the Lords to veto legislation was therefore removed since under the Act its assent is no longer required for the Bill to proceed for Royal Assent.

3. The Parliament Act 1949 reduced further the Lords' power of delay over non-Money Bills to one year.

4. In *R (Jackson) v Attorney-General* (2005) the Parliament Act 1949 was held to be valid and consequently any legislation passed under it (for example the Hunting Act 2004) is also valid.

5. The Parliament Acts have not been frequently used and the following are the only examples of use of the procedure:
   - the Government of Ireland Act 1914;
   - the Welsh Church Act 1914;
   - the War Crimes Act 1991;
   - the European Parliamentary Elections Act 1999;
   - the Sexual Offences (Amendment) Act 2000; and
   - the Hunting Act 2004.

6. One of the reasons why the procedure is infrequently resorted to is because of what is known as the 'Salisbury Convention'. This convention provides that the Lords will not insist on amendments unless the issue is very important and the electorate appears to approve the Lords' position. (For additional discussion of conventions see Chapter 2.)

5.5 Parliamentary privilege

5.5.1 The Bill of Rights 1688

1. Historically, the privileges of Parliament were derived from the rights asserted over the monarchy and were enshrined in the Bill of Rights 1688. These declared rights were a means to ensure that Parliament could go about its business without interference or undue influence.

2. At the opening of each parliamentary session, the Speaker announces and asserts these 'ancient and undoubted' rights and privileges. In a modern context, some privileges are of little importance, but the rules of parliamentary conduct remain significant. Because of the nature of these rules and the variance in application over time, it can be difficult to ascertain an exact definition of the rules, or to identify with certainty in what context they may be applied.

5.5.2 Freedom of speech

1. This is the most important freedom and in its modern context it protects MPs from legal actions arising from their words, written or spoken, in the course of carrying out their duties. It stems from Article 9 of the Bill of Rights. It can act as a shield to an action under the Official Secrets Acts, as in *Duncan Sandys' Case* (1938), or block jurisdiction for judicial review.

2. More frequently, the right of freedom of speech is used as a defence to a potential action in defamation, for example *Church of Scientology v Johnson-Smith* (1972).

3. The case of *Stockdale v Hansard* (1839) demonstrated that the courts will preserve their jurisdiction to determine the extent of privilege and try to protect the rights of individuals. But the case of *The Sheriff of Middlesex* (1840) which followed showed that the courts could not interfere with the House's ruling that a breach of privilege had been committed, even though no reasons were given.

4. Under Article 9 the protection from suit extends to words spoken or written in the course of **'proceedings in Parliament'**.

   (a) Because this term is not statutory, and has been interpreted over time, there is no clear definition of the types of speech or correspondence that will be protected.

   (b) In the *Strauss Affair* (1958) the question of the privileged or non-privileged status of a letter of complaint from a constituent to an MP arose. The Parliamentary Committee on Privilege considered that it did attract such privilege, but the House rejected this finding. The threat of suit was subsequently withdrawn.

5. Parliament amended the privilege of freedom of speech in the Defamation Act 1996. Section 13 of the Act allows an individual member to waive their privilege so that an action may be brought.

5.5.3 Absolute or qualified privilege

1. Absolute privilege extends to parliamentary proceedings and is a bar to all actions.

2. Qualified privilege may extend to newspaper or media reports, so long as the report is fair and accurate and malice cannot be demonstrated (*Wason v Walter* (1868)). For example:

   ● a parliamentary sketch may be privileged (*Cook v Alexander* (1974));

- a letter from an MP to the Lord Chancellor and Law Society may have qualified privilege (*Beech v Freeson* (1972)).

5.5.4 Privilege and the ECHR

1. In *A v UK* (2002) the applicant argued that the rules of privilege breached the Convention, in particular Article 6 (the right to a fair trial), Article 8 (respect for private life) and Article 13 (right to an effective remedy).
2. The European Court of Human Rights held that the rules of privilege were necessary to protect free speech in Parliament and there was no violation of the Convention. The Court also noted that the British rules were narrower in scope than in many other countries.

5.5.5 Self-regulation

The House has the right to regulate its own composition and its own proceedings. Hence:

- where a vacancy arises, the House orders a by-election;
- Parliament determines if a Member is qualified to take their seat in the House (*Re Parliamentary Election for Birstol South East* (1964));
- Parliament may expel a Member it considers unfit (*Bradlaugh v Gossett* (1884)); and
- Parliament may suspend a Member for improper conduct, e.g. in the case of a Member seizing the Mace in the course of a speech.

5.5.6 Residual privilege

1. Freedom from arrest for attending Members is of little significance, since it does not prevent an arrest for a criminal charge and there are few arrestable civil offences.
2. An example of such arrest arose from *Stourton v Stourton* (1963), which concerned maintenance arrears.

5.5.7 Contempt of Parliament

Parliament judges whether conduct is such that it amounts to contempt. Such conduct could include, for example:
- misleading a House or a Committee;
- forgery of documents;
- corruption by bribery; and
- molesting, intimidating or otherwise interfering with Members in the course of their work in Parliament.

5.5.8 Members' interests

1. Privilege is based upon the concept of Parliament being free to operate without fear or favour and this requires that its Members be above corruption and influence. It has long been accepted that bodies may sponsor MPs, such as trade unions, but there has been concern, with regard to both Labour and Conservative Governments, that certain contributions or gifts amounted to bribes. The Political Parties, Elections and Referendums Act 2000 (see 5.2.4 above) contains measures to combat this to some extent.
2. The **Register of Members' Interests** is designed to be an open record of all MPs' consultancies and allegiances, as well as revealing any financial benefits and benefits in kind. Unfortunately, MPs have not always been scrupulous in keeping the Register up to date.
3. The **Committee on Standards in Public Life** (the Nolan Committee) was convened, following the cash for questions affair, to report on all aspects of MPs' financial interests. The Committee published its report in 1995, which concluded that interests outside Parliament should not be banned but that the Register should be kept more assiduously. It also concluded that the rules on required disclosures of financial and other interests be clarified.
4. In response to the Report the House approved a **Code of Conduct**. The Code sets out general principles to guide standards of conduct and use of the Register.

5. MPs must now:
- notify any contracts where they act in a parliamentary capacity on behalf of any organisation;
- disclose their annual remuneration;
- disclose any monetary benefits of any kind; and
- disclose, whenever they approach another Member or Minister, any financial interest they may have in the subject at hand.

6. Paid advocacy is banned in relation to:
- initiating parliamentary proceedings;
- presentation of petitions;
- asking parliamentary questions;
- tabling or moving motions; and
- moving amendments to Bills.

7. The office of Parliamentary Commissioner was introduced to advise MPs and to investigate allegations in respect of the Register of Members' Interests and complaints of breaches of the Code of Conduct. The Commissioner reports to the Standards and Privileges Committee; the Committee may examine the matter and reports to the House of Commons, which makes any final decision in respect of the matter.

5.5.10 Penalties

1. To a certain extent, the House determines penalties for breach of privilege. It no longer uses the power of imprisonment and its power to issue fines seems to have lapsed. The House can recommend prosecution or call upon the Sarjeant-at-Arms to expel a troublemaker. Most commonly, in the case of Members, a reprimand is issued or a period of suspension ordered.

2. Some examples of the imposition of penalties for breach of privilege/contempt of Parliament include:
- 1948 – Gary Allighan MP was expelled for lying to a Committee;

- 1988 – Ron Brown MP was suspended for damaging the Mace;
- 1994 – two MPs were suspended, with loss of pay, for taking money to put down parliamentary questions;
- 2004 – a Labour Minister was required to apologise to the House for not registering earnings;
- 2009 – Derek Conway MP was ordered by the Standard and Privileges Committee to repay £3,700 of public money paid to his son for 'research work' and to apologise to the House; and
- 2009 – John McDonnell MP was suspended for five days for picking up and moving the Mace.

CHAPTER 6

Executive Accountability

Cabinet and the Prime Minister

CONVENTIONS OF MINISTERIAL RESPONSIBILITY

Collective ministerial responsibility
- Definition
- Rules

Individual ministerial responsibility
- Ministerial Code
- Personal conduct

SCRUTINY OF THE EXECUTIVE
Parliament
Debates; Question Time; Select Committees
Parliamentary Commissioner for Standards
Parliamentary Commissioner for Administration
Other controls

PREROGATIVE POWERS
Definition; significance; examples
Limitations
Judicial review – *GCHQ* (1985); *ex parte Rees-Mogg* (1994); *ex parte Bentley* (1994); *ex parte Everett* (1989); *CND v PM* (2002); *ex parte P* (1995); *Bancoult* (2008)
Statute – *De Keysers* (1920); *Laker Airways v Secretary of State for Trade* (1977); *ex parte FBU* (1995)
Reform
Draft Constitutional Renewal Bill

6.1 Cabinet and the Prime Minister

6.1.1 The office of Prime Minister

1. The office of Prime Minister (PM) is a historical creation. It has no statutory basis save for the provision of a salary (Ministerial and Other Salaries Act 1975). The first individual to occupy what we now regard as the PM post was William Walpole.
2. By the 1830s a structure of ministerial government with departmental responsibilities, under the leadership of an elected party leader, was established.
3. The PM today retains personal control of many key responsibilities of government, which can be exercised under the prerogative (see 6.4), for example:
   - the right to nominate the Government;
   - the right to request the dissolution of Parliament;
   - the control of the Cabinet agenda;
   - selection of the Lord Chancellor;
   - chair of Cabinet Committees.
4. The question most commonly raised with regard to the PM is the extent to which such a concentration of power in the hands of one individual is appropriate in a democracy, and whether there are sufficient controls on the exercise of this power.

6.1.2 The Cabinet

1. The Cabinet in its modern form is derived from the ancient circle of advisers to the monarch. It was not until the 19th century that clear areas of ministerial responsibility at Cabinet level emerged.
2. The modern Cabinet is selected by the PM; typically, its membership numbers around 20. In addition to the Lord Chancellor (Secretary of State for Constitutional Affairs) and the Chancellor of the Exchequer, each post represents a Department of State designated as the PM determines.

3. The Cabinet functions as a policy forum and as a means of co-ordinating departmental strategies.
4. A key criticism of modern Cabinets is the extent to which they have become a 'rubber stamp' for policy-making by the PM rather than a collective decision-making body.
5. The Cabinet's timetable of meetings is determined by the PM. There is no requirement that a full Cabinet take key decisions. For example:
   - Thatcher controversially took decisions in the Westland Affair and the Falklands War without summoning a full Cabinet;
   - Attlee approved the development of a nuclear bomb at a meeting to which two Cabinet Ministers were refused access.
6. There are typically 12 to 14 standing Cabinet Committees, as well as a number of *ad hoc* committees dedicated to departmental affairs.

6.2 The conventions of ministerial responsibility

1. According to the rule of law (see Chapter 3) it is essential that government is responsible for its actions. A responsible government is one that is both accountable and responsive to Parliament and to the electorate.
2. Under the UK constitution this is not secured by formal or legal rules but by convention (see Chapter 2).
3. The conventions include:
   - collective ministerial responsibility; and
   - individual ministerial responsibility.
4. Individual ministerial responsibility includes both departmental responsibility and responsibility for personal conduct.

6.2.1 Collective ministerial responsibility

1. Whilst the Cabinet is at the core of government and has extensive powers, the doctrine of collective responsibility is a reminder that Parliament remains sovereign and that the Cabinet must answer to Parliament for its actions and inactions.

2. The classic definition of the convention of collective ministerial responsibility is that of Lord Salisbury in 1878: 'For all that passes in Cabinet every member of it who does not resign is absolutely and irretrievably responsible and has no right afterwards to say that he agreed in one case to a compromise, while in another he was persuaded by his colleagues'.

3. The convention is justified by the need for the government to present a united front to maintain public confidence, hence the government as a whole should resign if defeated in a vote of no confidence or if the PM resigns.

4. There are two rules under the convention (which are also expressed in the Ministerial Code 2007):
   - under the **unanimity rule**, once agreement is reached in the Cabinet all members are bound to speak in support of the decision in public, regardless of whether they agreed or were present; and
   - under the **confidentiality rule**, all formal records of Cabinet meetings are protected under the Parliamentary Papers Act 1970 '30-year rule' unless disclosure is permitted by the PM. Non-official accounts, such as memoirs, are subject to the principle set out in *Attorney-General v Jonathan Cape Ltd* (1976). (A review of the 30-year rule has recently been undertaken. In the report published in January 2009, the recommendation to the Government was to reduce the rule to 15 years.)

5. Examples of ministerial resignations because Ministers felt unable to abide by the unanimity rule include:
   - 1986 – Michael Heseltine, Secretary of State for Trade and Industry, resigned over the Westland Helicopter incident; and

● 1990 – Geoffrey Howe resigned over EC policy.

6. Resignations on the basis of a breakdown in the ability of the Cabinet to maintain a united front can result in considerable embarrassment for the Government. For example, the above resignation of Geoffrey Howe was considered extremely influential in ending Margaret Thatcher's Prime Ministership.

7. In practice, the above rules should operate to protect a Minister under attack for a policy, decision etc. because their colleagues should help defend them. However, this may not be effective if the media is determined to pursue the matter and/or the Minister loses the support of the PM, which could force their resignation.

8. The convention is flexible and can be relaxed by the PM where in extreme circumstances agreement cannot be reached. For example, in 1975 the PM, Harold Wilson, waived the convention in respect of the UK's continued membership of the then EEC prior to a referendum.

6.2.2 Individual ministerial responsibility

1. This convention places Ministers in a position of having to answer for the work of their departments. The doctrine is identified with the *Carltona* principle (*Carltona Ltd v Works Commissioners* (1943)), which provides that a decision taken by a junior/subordinate official is regarded as being the decision of the Minister in charge of the department and they must answer for it in Parliament.

2. Ministers are also responsible for the actions of civil servants, according to the principles set out in the *Crichel Down Affair* (1953).

3. According to *Crichel Down*, the Minister is responsible if the civil servant is following direct instruction and/or policy.

4. The modern basis for ministerial responsibility is now found in the **Ministerial Code**. This states that:

● Ministers have a duty to Parliament to account for the policies, decisions and actions of their Departments and

Next Step Agencies (see Chapter 7 for further discussion);

- Ministers must give accurate and truthful information and correct errors at the earliest opportunity. Ministers that knowingly mislead are expected to offer their resignation to the PM;
- Ministers should be as open as possible with Parliament, refusing to disclose information only when not in the public interest;
- Ministers should require civil servants who give evidence on their behalf to parliamentary committee under their direction to be as helpful as possible in providing accurate, truthful and full information;
- Ministers must ensure that no conflict arises, or appears to arise, between their public duties and their private interests.

5. However, the Code has no legal force and there is no independent method of enforcing it; the Parliamentary Commissioner for Standards cannot investigate alleged breaches of the Code by Ministers.

6. Instead the Code states that Ministers remain in office only as long as they have the confidence of the PM. It is therefore the PM that is 'the ultimate judge of the standards of behaviour expected of a Minister and the appropriate consequences of a breach of those standards'.

7. Between 1954 and 1982 there were no ministerial resignations following departmental misadministration, even though there were clear instances of such having occurred. In 1982, Lord Carrington and two other Ministers resigned over allegations that British forces were not prepared when Argentina invaded the Falklands.

8. Other examples of ministerial responses to accepting or not accepting responsibility include:
   - 1989 – Edwina Currie, junior Health Minister, resigned over the salmonella in eggs scandal; she consistently refused to attend the select committee investigation (see

below) and after attracting much negative media attention lost the support of the PM.

- 1994 – Michael Howard, then Home Secretary, refused to resign after a number of prison escapes. He made a distinction between 'policy' matters, for which he was responsible, and 'operational' matters, for which he claimed he was not responsible.
- 2002 – Stephen Byers, Secretary of State for Transport, resigned after failing to progress transport policy and misleading Parliament on the abolition of Railtrack (failure to dismiss an adviser for an e-mail remark about 9/11 did not help his position).
- 2002 – Estelle Morris, Secretary of State for Education, resigned for the maladministration of A-level results that year.
- 2004 – Beverley Hughes resigned after it was established that she was wrong in denying knowledge of the scale of bogus visa applications.

9. It appears that, in the case of responsibility for departmental maladministration or mismanagement, there are no clear rules on when a Minister should resign but three influential factors:

- whether they continue to have the support of the PM (e.g. Tessa Jowell and Charles Clark in 2006);
- whether they continue to have the support of their party;
- the extent of negative media attention and the loss of public support; even if they have the above initially this factor may lead to the loss of such support.

10. There are suggestions that the process of securing the responsibility of both Ministers and MPs has improved with the development of and/or increased use of the following:

- better enforcement and clarification of the use of the Register of Members' Interests (see Chapter 5);
- the Advisory Committee on Business Appointments;

- the Standards and Privileges Committee; and
- the Parliamentary Commissioner for Standards (see below at 6.3.2).

6.2.3 The personal conduct of Ministers

1. There are no provisions requiring Ministers to hold particular qualifications or a formal vetting process to identify their appropriateness to hold public office; appointment is purely at the discretion of the PM (see for example the decisions to re-appoint David Blunkett and Peter Mandelson) and, as with individual ministerial responsibility for departmental administration, the support of the PM can be very influential.

2. Personal conduct may lead to resignation, and indeed seemingly more so than in cases where there is acceptance of departmental responsibility.

3. We can see examples of such resignations in the context of personal relationships and the holding of private financial interests.

   a) **Personal relationships**

   - 1963 – John Profumo, Minister of Defence, resigned after he was found to have had a relationship with a prostitute, who was also having a relationship with a Russian naval attaché.
   - 1983 – Cecil Parkinson, Secretary of State for Trade and Industry, resigned after it was revealed that he had a pregnant mistress.
   - 1992 – David Mellor, Heritage Secretary, resigned after it was revealed he was having a relationship with an actress and for receiving gifts including the hospitality of a Palestinian Liberation Organisation official.
   - 1998 – Ron Davies, Welsh Secretary, resigned after an incident on Clapham Common.
   - 2004 – David Blunkett, Home Secretary, resigned after it was disclosed he had fast-tracked an application for his mistress's nanny to stay in the UK.

b) Private financial interests

1. The Ministerial Code 2007 provides that Ministers 'must scrupulously avoid any danger of an actual or apparent conflict of interest between their Ministerial position and their private financial interests'.

2. Ministers are required to
   - declare their financial interests in the Register of Members' Interests (see Chapter 5); and
   - consult the Advisory Committee on Business Appointments on any business appointments they intend to take up within two years of leaving office.

3. The Code no longer requires Ministers to resign any directorships they hold on assuming office, although if a Minister does have a financial interest they must not be involved in any decision-making relating to it.

4. Examples of dishonesty in respect of financial interests leading to resignation include:
   - 1992 – Norman Lamont, Chancellor of the Exchequer, resigned after receiving public money for legal fees.
   - 1993 – Michael Mates, Minister for Northern Ireland, was alleged to have accepted the loan of a car from an individual facing prosecution on charges of theft and fraud.
   - 1998 – Peter Mandelson, Secretary of State for Trade and Industry, resigned after it was disclosed he had accepted a personal loan from Geoffrey Robertson, the Paymaster General, who also resigned (Mandelson was forced to resign again a year later after interfering in the passport application of an Indian businessman who had contributed to the Millennium Dome building).
   - 2005 – David Blunkett, Work and Pensions Secretary, was forced to resign for the second time after failing to consult the Advisory Committee on Business Appointments.

6.3 Scrutiny of the executive

1. To ensure executive accountability and responsibility, and consequently the operation of the conventions of ministerial responsibility, is Parliament's most constitutionally significant role.
2. Parliament in the form of both houses has at its disposal a number of mechanisms to scrutinise executive action.

6.3.1 Debates

1. Debates take place at various stages as a Bill proceeds through Parliament. The most in-depth debate of proposed legislation takes place at the second reading. The debates that take place at the report stage are generally more brief, although there have been exceptions to this (e.g. Police and Criminal Evidence Act 1984).
2. Any MP, or group of MPs, may request an Early Day Motion, which is a written motion tabled in Parliament for a debate on any subject-matter.
3. At the end of the parliamentary day backbenchers may initiate short debates on matters of their choice known as Daily Adjournment debates. These involve the MP speaking for 15 minutes and the relevant Minister being able to respond for 15 minutes.
4. Any MP can apply to the Speaker for an emergency debate, which will be a three-hour debate held the following day.
5. The effectiveness of debates in the House of Commons as a means of scrutinising the executive is varied and can depend on a number of factors, including:
   - the size of the Government's majority;
   - the strength and experience of the opposition parties; and
   - whether backbenchers are prepared to challenge the Government.
6. Debates can also take place in the House of Lords. Debates in this House have traditionally had a good reputation as being well-informed with reduced party influence.

6.3.2 Question Time

1. Question Time takes place on Mondays, Tuesdays and Thursdays between 2.35 pm and 3.30 pm. The Government provides a rota so that different Ministers answer questions during these periods.

2. Answers to questions can be requested in either oral or written format. However, not all oral questions can be answered within parliamentary time, in which case a written answer is provided.

3. The oral question process includes the ability of an MP to ask a supplementary question, for which no notice has to be given.

4. Urgent oral questions can be raised for immediate discussion after Question Time but must be approved by the Speaker by noon on the day the question is to be asked. The Speaker has discretion as to whether to permit it.

5. Question Time can be effective in that it achieves a great deal of publicity and the responses, whether oral or written, being published, can provide a wealth of information. However, there are also a number of limitations.

6. Rules have been created, enforced by the Speaker, which limit the range of questions that can be asked. The following matters cannot be part of Question Time:
   - matters pertaining to the monarch;
   - certain matters of the prerogative; and
   - questions that do not relate to the responsibility of the individual Minister.

7. There is also a wide range of subjects that questions cannot be asked on, including:
   - local authorities;
   - personal powers of the monarch;
   - internal affairs of other countries;
   - defence and national security;
   - Cabinet business;
   - advice given to Ministers by civil servants;
   - nationalised industries; and
   - matters that are *sub judice*.

8. The Speaker will also reject questions that are:
- too broad to be answered within the time constraints;
- trivial or irrelevant;
- critical of the judiciary; and
- not phrased in proper parliamentary language.

9. In addition to the above limitations:
- answers to questions may be refused because of their disproportionate cost;
- urgent questions are often made to the Speaker but very few are accepted; and
- notice of three sitting days must be given which, although justified on the basis of giving Ministers appropriate time to prepare, significantly reduces the spontaneity of the process.

6.3.3 Prime Minister's Question Time

1. This takes place on Wednesdays and lasts for 30 minutes.
2. The process requires the asking of an 'open' question before the MP may ask up to two supplementary questions.
3. The supplementary questions can be on any matter for which the PM is responsible, or matters that fall outside the responsibility of an individual Minister.
4. The Leader of the Opposition can ask up to six questions on almost any aspect of governmental policy.
5. Prime Minister's Question Time is televised and attracts considerable attention. Its effectiveness is enhanced by the fact that there is no advance notice of the questions to be asked.

6.3.4 Select committees

1. The current system of departmentally related select committees was created in 1979. Their functions are to examine matters within Government Departments and to report to the House of Commons.

2. Select committees have discretion on what matters to investigate and the evidence required. They have the power to call for persons, papers and records. They can also appoint specialist advisers.

3. Membership of select committees is of a cross-party nature but is reflective of the strength of each party in the House. According to convention, they are largely made up of backbenchers.

4. However, select committees do not have the power to compel Ministers to give evidence (although failure to do so may amount to contempt of Parliament) and there can be difficulties in securing governmental and other co-operation. For example:

   • 1988 – Edwina Currie refused to attend the Select Committee on Agriculture to give evidence after her remarks on salmonella in eggs caused considerable damage to the egg industry.

   • 1991/2 – the Social Services Select Committee was investigating the mismanagement of pension funds by the deceased Robert Maxwell. It invited his sons to give evidence since they had assumed control of the company. Whilst they attended, they refused to answer any questions.

   • 1992 – the Select Committee on Trade and Industry was examining the granting of export licences for the sale of equipment to Iraq during the Gulf War. The Attorney-General and others refused to attend and give evidence on the information held at the time by the Department of Trade and Industry.

5. Another potential limitation on the effectiveness of select committees is that only approximately one third of reports produced are debated in the House of Commons. This is a reflection of the considerable pressure on parliamentary time. Reports are, though, published and therefore provide considerable and extensive information that is in the public domain.

6.3.5 Parliamentary Commissioner for Standards

1. The office of Parliamentary Commissioner for Standards was introduced following the 'cash for questions' affair and the resulting report of the Committee on Standards in Public Life (the Nolan Report). Their role is to advise MPs and to investigate allegations in respect of the Register of Members' Interests (see Chapter 5) and complaints of breaches of the Code of Conduct.

2. The Commissioner reports to the Committee for Standards and Privileges, which may examine the matter. It in turn reports to the House of Commons, which makes the final decision on the matter.

3. The Commissioner, however, does not investigate the conduct of Ministers since the Ministerial Code is enforced by the PM.

6.3.6 Parliamentary Commissioner for Administration

1. The Parliamentary Commissioner for Administration (or ombudsman), a post created under the Parliamentary Commissioner Act 1967, is appointed by the Crown on the advice of the Government. Their role is to:
   - consider and resolve complaints impartially;
   - report results to complainants impartially; and
   - promote improvements in public services.

2. Under s 5(1) of the Parliamentary Commissioner Act 1967, a member of the public may make a complaint if they 'have sustained injustice in consequence of maladministration'. The complaint must be made in writing to the relevant constituency MP within 12 months and can only relate to maladministration, not the merits of a decision or policy.

3. The Commissioner has discretion as to whether to accept a complaint. The exercise of this discretion is subject to judicial review: *R v Parliamentary Commissioner for Administration, ex parte Dyer* (1994). (See Chapters 11 and 12 for detail on judicial review.)
4. There are limitations on the effectiveness of the Commissioner, primarily:
   a) the requirement that the complaint be made to an MP and not directly to the Commissioner;
   b) the range of excluded matters that the Commissioner cannot investigate. These include the work of the following:
      - the police;
      - Cabinet Office;
      - PM's Office;
      - Parole Board;
      - tribunals;
      - Bank of England;
      - Criminal Injuries Compensation Board; and
      - nationalised industries.
   c) The Commissioner cannot investigate where the complainant has a right of appeal or review, unless it would be unreasonable for them to resort to such a remedy; and
   d) The Commissioner cannot investigate a range of government departmental matters including:
      - action by the Secretary of State in respect of investigating crime or matters of national security;
      - dealings with other governments and international organisations;
      - the granting of honours, awards or privileges;
      - personnel matters in respect of the armed forces and other Crown employment; and
      - exercise of the prerogative of mercy.

6.3.7 Other controls

1. In addition to the above, there are a range of other bodies and/or mechanisms that may secure the accountability of the executive. In brief these include:

a) **Judicial review**: operating under the rule of law, judicial review can be extremely effective in securing the accountability of the executive. However, there can be some difficulty in securing an effective remedy (see Chapters 11 and 12).

b) **The media**: good-quality investigative journalism can generate public awareness of Government and/or individual deficiencies, maladministration etc. In some cases this can be limited, by, for example, libel laws, but freedom of expression is a ECHR right (see Chapter 9).

c) **The electorate**: free elections provide the public or electorate with the opportunity to elect a different political party into power, thereby showing its dissatisfaction with a previous administration. The effectiveness of this is however limited by a range of factors including: the fact that the PM decides the timing of a General Election; the method of voting, the first past the post system, can disenfranchise the electorate (see Chapter 5); and the process often results in large Government majorities.

6.4 The royal prerogative

6.4.1 Definition and significance

1. The royal prerogative is a source of constitutional law (see Chapter 2). It derives from common law powers that have transferred from the monarchy to the executive, which is discussed below.

2. The significance in constitutional law of the prerogative is that it provides the executive with considerable power to act without following 'normal' parliamentary procedures. As Dicey explained, the prerogative is 'every act which the executive government can lawfully do without the authority of an Act of Parliament'.

3. No new prerogative powers can be created according to the case of *Entick v Carrington* (1765). (See also *BBC v Johns* (1965).)

6.4.2 The personal prerogatives of the monarch

1. Prerogative powers originated in the powers of the monarch, who could act in their own inherent right.
2. The monarch's powers included:
   - appointment and dismissal of Ministers;
   - law-making by proclamation;
   - establishing Royal Courts without judges;
   - raising taxation;
   - deploying forces in defence of the realm;
   - immunity from suit; and
   - the grant of honours.

6.4.3 Challenges to the power of the monarch

1. By the reign of James I (1603–25) the monarch was faced with an increasingly effective Parliament, culminating in the temporary abolition of the monarchy in 1625. Consequently, the monarchy's powers were eroded by both revolution and by legal challenges, including the following:
   - *Case of Proclamations* (1611) – the monarch could not change the law by proclamation. The law of the land, which required that law be made by Parliament, limited the prerogative;
   - *Prohibitions Del Roy* (1607) – the monarch had no right to act as a judge;
   - *The Ship Money Case* (1637) – although the court declared it to be within the monarch's power to determine a state of emergency, requiring tax raising, the Ship Money Act 1637 was passed, making it illegal for

the monarch to raise taxation;

- The Bill of Rights 1688 – crystallised the transfer of power from the monarchy to Parliament and the restoration of the monarchy under the legal control of Parliament.

2. Certain prerogative powers remain in the hands of the monarch to the present day but convention requires that the monarch act only on the advice of Government Ministers. Hence, in theory, the monarch may appoint and dismiss Ministers and veto legislation by refusing the Royal Assent, yet in practice these prerogatives are now exercised by the Government.

6.4.4 Modern prerogative powers

1. Modern prerogative powers may be defined as the legal powers inherent in Government, which do not require the approval of Parliament for their exercise.

2. All prerogative powers are derived from those original powers of the monarch, though in a modern context they are extensive and a non-exhaustive list would include the following examples:

Foreign Affairs
Disposition of armed forces
Treaty making
Declaration of war and peace
Recognition of foreign states and governments
International diplomatic relations
Granting passports

Domestic Affairs
Summoning and dissolution of Parliament
Royal Assent
Appointment of Ministers

Judicial
Halting criminal prosecutions
Granting mercy
Pardoning and reducing sentences
Power of Attorney-General to represent the Crown

---

3. The significance for constitutional law is the extent to which these extensive powers are scrutinised and controlled.

6.4.5 Limitations to the exercise of prerogative powers

There are a number of limitations on the exercise of prerogative powers.

1. Royal prerogative and the courts

- The exercise of prerogative powers was originally not susceptible to judicial review. (For detail on judicial review see Chapters 11 and 12.)
- However, since the landmark judgment in *CCSU v Minister for the Civil Service* (1985) (otherwise known as *GCHQ*) the exercise of certain prerogative powers is now capable of being reviewed by the courts.
- However, only certain prerogatives are capable of being reviewed by the courts. Whether a prerogative power is susceptible to judicial review will depend on its nature/ subject-matter.
- Lord Diplock in the *GCHQ* Case (1985) suggested that ministerial decisions exercising prerogative powers could be difficult to challenge because they would 'generally involve the application of government policy'. In other words, they would be non-justiciable prerogative powers.
- Lord Roskill identified some non-justiciable prerogative powers in the *GCHQ* Case, including:
  - making treaties;
  - defence of the realm;

- – prerogative of mercy;
- – granting honours;
- – dissolution of Parliament; and
- – appointment of Ministers.
- Since the *GCHQ* Case, however, the courts have appeared willing to examine a range of prerogative powers, including some of the below.

Example: Treaty making powers

In *R v Secretary of State for Foreign and Commonwealth Affairs, ex parte Rees-Mogg* (1994) the Court of Appeal discussed the prerogative of treaty-making but concluded it was a non-reviewable power.

Example: Mercy/Pardons

This prerogative was traditionally non-reviewable (*DeFreitas v Benny* (1976)) but in *R v Secretary of State for the Home Department, ex parte Bentley* (1994) the court considered 'some aspects' of the prerogative of mercy to be reviewable. The court did not make any formal order in the case but invited the Home Secretary to reconsider the issues. In 1998 the Criminal Cases Review Commission referred the case to the Court of Appeal, where the conviction was held unsafe and quashed (see also *Attorney-General of Trinidad and Tobago v Lennox Phillips* (1995)).

Example: Issuing passports

In *R v Secretary of State for Foreign and Commonwealth Affairs, ex parte Everett* (1989) the Court of Appeal held the issuing of passports to be a reviewable prerogative on the basis that it is a 'matter of administrative decision, affecting the rights of individuals and their freedom of travel': see also *R v Secretary of State for the Home Department, ex parte Al-Fayed* (1997).

Example: Declaring war and deployment of troops

In *Campaign for Nuclear Disarmament v PM* (2002), CND

challenged the decision of the Government to send troops to Iraq. This was considered to be a 'classic example' of a non-reviewable prerogative power.

Example: Power to make *ex gratia* payments

In *R v Criminal Compensation Board and Another, ex parte P* (1995) the prerogative power of making *ex gratia* payments to the victims of crime was held to be reviewable. In *National Farmers Union v Secretary of State for the Environment, Food and Rural Affairs* (2003), the NFU was able to challenge *ex gratia* payments made to farmers on the culling of their livestock as a result of the foot and mouth epidemic.

Example: Defence of the realm

Considered non-reviewable in *GCHQ*, even this prerogative has in certain contexts been scrutinised by the courts, aided by the passing of the Human Rights Act 1998. For example, in *A (FC) v Secretary of State for the Home Department* (2005) the House of Lords set aside a derogation order made on the grounds of State emergency as being disproportionate to the objective.

Example: Orders in Council

In *R (Bancoult) v Secretary of State for Foreign and Commonwealth Affairs* (2008) the House of Lords held that prerogative Orders in Council do not share all of the characteristics of an Act of Parliament, and that an exercise of the prerogative in such a way could be subject to judicial review.

2. Royal prerogative and statute

- Because of the doctrine of parliamentary supremacy, legislation in the form of statute has overtaken large areas of the prerogative. For example, the prerogative of issuing warrants for telephone tapping was replaced by the Regulation of Investigatory Powers Act 2000.

- If the royal prerogative and statute exist on the same subject-matter the prerogative power must be suspended: *AG v De Keyser's Royal Hotel Ltd* (1920).
- Prerogative powers can only be used in such circumstances if the statute **expressly** provides so. If this is the case any subsequent use of the prerogative power must conform to the terms of the statute: *Laker Airways v Secretary of State for Trade* (1977).
- A Minister must also not seek to rely on prerogative powers to create new regulations in order to override statutory provisions according to the case of *R v Secretary of State for the Home Department, ex parte Fire Brigades Union* (1995).

3. **Extending the range of prerogative powers**
   - The case of *Entick v Carrington* (1765) determined that the range of prerogative powers was at that date closed – in other words, that no new prerogative powers could be created. This was confirmed 200 years later in *BBC v Johns* (1965).
   - It appears that an established prerogative may be exercised in a new or modern context where it is a logical inference from the powers conferred: *R v Secretary of State for the Home Department, ex parte Northumbria Police Authority* (1988).
   - It should be noted, however, that drawing the line between using an existing prerogative in a new or modern context and creating what is in effect a new prerogative is a thin one. The constitutional issue is therefore the potential for the executive to abuse such powers yet justify such action on the basis that it is merely the exercise of an existing prerogative in a new context.

6.4.6 Reform of the prerogative

1. The draft Constitutional Renewal Bill was put before Parliament in the 2007–08 session. It makes proposals to

reform some important prerogative powers so that the executive is more accountable in their use. These reforms include:

- **ratification of international treaties** – the proposals are to formalise the procedure for Parliament to scrutinise treaties so that consent will only be provided once a treaty has been laid before Parliament for 21 sitting days. This would codify existing convention, known as the 'Ponsonby Rule'. In addition, it is proposed that a vote against ratification by the House of Commons should have legal effect. However, these proposals fall short of a statutory requirement for Parliament's approval prior to ratification.
- **deployment of armed troops** – there is a proposal to, by House of Commons resolution, allow Parliament a substantive vote before UK troops are deployed in military action. However, the Government will retain sufficient powers so that it can deploy for reasons of urgency or necessary operational security.
- **Civil Service** – there are additional proposals to enshrine in statute the core values of the Civil Service and reform appointments. These will be discussed in the following chapter.

CHAPTER 7

The Civil Service and Open Government

THE CIVIL SERVICE

↓

Definition

↓

Constitutional principles
Permanency, neutrality, anonymity

↓

Civil Service Code
Integrity, honesty, objectivity, impartiality

↓

Traditional accountability

↓

Difficulties in ensuring accountability
Next Steps Agencies
Special Advisers

↓

Reform
Draft Constitutional Renewal Bill

OPEN GOVERNMENT

The Freedom of Information Act 2000

↓

Effectiveness – exempt information

7.1 The Civil Service

7.1.1 The definition of a civil servant

1. A civil servant is a servant of the Crown but not holder of political or judicial office, who is employed in a civil capacity and whose remuneration is paid wholly and directly from monies voted by Parliament.

2. It is extremely difficult to assess the number of civil servants, primarily because of problems in defining whether particular roles are within the public service. The size of a civil service staff for a department will depend on its relative size.

3. The terms and conditions of a civil servant's employment are regulated under the prerogative (see Chapter 6).

7.1.2 Constitutional principles and the Civil Service

Traditionally, under constitutional principles, the Civil Service displays three characteristics:

1. Permanency

Civil servants hold permanent posts. This is justified on the basis that expertise can develop and be maintained from one government to the next. This is in contrast to other constitutions where the Civil Service is semi-permanent and senior posts change with a change of government, such as in the USA.

2. Political neutrality

The Civil Service must be loyal to the government of the day, regardless of which political party it is comprised of. This is justified on the basis of ensuring a lack of political bias. There has though been constant criticism of whether the Civil Service is indeed politically neutral.

3. Anonymity

The Civil Service is traditionally anonymous and protected from public enquiry – instead the Minister should be seen to be responsible and accountable. This is justified as a means of ensuring impartiality.

7.1.3 The Civil Service Code

The Code states that the core values of the Civil Service are:

- **integrity** – to put the obligations of public service over personal interests;
- **honesty** – to be truthful and open;
- **objectivity** – to base advice and decisions on rigorous analysis of the evidence; and
- **impartiality** – to act solely according to the merits of the case and serve governments of different political persuasion equally.

7.1.4 Traditional principles of accountability

1. The Civil Service is not accountable to Parliament, thereby protecting its anonymity. Instead, by convention, it is the Minister in charge of the particular government department that is responsible to Parliament for the conduct of civil servants.
2. The Minister is obligated to:
   - explain and answer for the work of their department to Parliament; and
   - take responsibility for any failure of departmental policy or administration (see Chapter 6 for further details).

7.1.5 Difficulties in ensuring accountability

1. Ensuring accountability has become increasingly difficult for a number of reasons:
   a) departments have massively increased in size, to the extent that it could be questioned whether the Minister is indeed making decisions;

b) Ministers change on an increasingly frequent basis, with numerous Cabinet reshuffles;

c) at a practical level the work of a Minister means that they spend what has been estimated to be only one third of their time on departmental business; and

d) the proliferation of government agencies and creation of quangos. Hence Ministers are distanced from operational matters.

2. Government agencies came as a result of attempts to improve the efficiency of the Civil Service ('Next Steps') in the late 1980s. Such agencies include the Benefits Agency; Child Support Agency; Driver and Vehicle Licensing Agency; and UK Passport Agency.

3. Each agency has independence in how it meets its objectives. There is a Head of Agency who should be directly responsible for operational matters, whilst the Minister remains responsible for policy (see the Ministerial Code discussed in Chapter 6). Ministers are therefore no longer expected to have an in-depth knowledge of operations on a day-to-day basis.

4. More recently there has been a move towards privatising previously state bodies so that they become non-departmental public bodies or quangos. A number of bodies have been sold into private ownership including British Rail and British Telecom. Questions remain on the extent to which Ministers exert control over such bodies and whether Parliament can secure their accountability for the way in which such bodies implement policy.

5. Government Ministers have also increasingly appointed 'Special Advisers' (e.g. Alastair Campbell). These are Crown servants and temporary civil servants, and paid from public funds, but not formally part of any department.

6. The Code of Conduct for Special Advisers states that special advisers are to help Ministers on matters 'where the work of Government and the work of the Government Party overlap' and it would be inappropriate for permanent civil servants to become involved.

7. The code describes the types of work they do as including:
   - reviewing ministerial papers and giving advice on departmental business;
   - checking facts and research findings from a party viewpoint;
   - preparing policy papers and contributing to party planning within a department;
   - liaising with the party;
   - briefing party MPs and officials on issues of government policy;
   - liaising with outside interest groups;
   - speechwriting;
   - representing the views of the ministers to the media where authorised to do so;
   - providing expert advice as a specialist in a particular field;
   - attending party functions; and
   - participating in party reiews organised by the party.

8. Special advisers should, according to the code, act with integrity and honesty but are exempt from the general rule to be impartial and objective. They should not misuse their position to:
   - further private interests;
   - receive benefits of a compromising nature;
   - disclose official information communicated in confidence; or
   - use official resources for party political activity.

9. However, there are accusations that the increasing use of special advisers has 'politicised' the Civil Service and that there is insufficient scrutiny and control over their activities (see below).

7.1.6 Reform of the Civil Service

1. The draft Constitutional Renewal Bill, which was put before Parliament in its 2007–08 session, proposes reform of the Civil Service.

2. The core values of the Civil Service identified as impartiality, integrity, honesty and objectivity will be enshrined in statute.

3. The PM (who is Minister for the Civil Service) appoints civil servants under the prerogative. Such appointments are historically made on 'merit' but this will be enshrined in statute along with the need for appointments to be based on fair and open competition.

4. The role and powers of special advisers will be clarified and formalised. The demand for scrutiny and reform of the role of special advisers has grown as a consequence of the resignation of Damian McBride following the 'e-mail smear' scandal in April 2009.

7.2 Open government

7.2.1 The need for legislation

1. For many years there were increasing demands for more open government and a right to access information. In 1997 the new Labour Government promised to generate greater openness and produced the Freedom of Information Act 2000, which applied to central government from November 2002 and which came into force fully in 2005.

2. The Act replaced the Code of Practice on Access to Government Information and amended the Data Protection Act 1998 and the Public Records Act 1958 (see below).

3. Under section 1, the Act created a legal right for citizens to access data held by public authorities including local government, National Health Service bodies, school, colleges and the police.

4. Requests for information must be in writing; the body receiving the request is obligated to reply within 20 working days of its receipt. A fee must be paid and the duty to disclose the information does not arise until that fee is paid.

5. A public authority may refuse to disclose information where the costs exceed prescribed limits.

6. The Act is regulated by a Commissioner who has investigative and enforcement powers.

7.2.2 The effectiveness of the Act

1. The effectiveness of the Act is weakened by a list of exempted information. There are two categories – information that is absolutely exempt and information that requires examination to see whether it is in the public interest to disclose it.
2. The following is information exempt from disclosure:
   (a) information that is accessible by using other means;
   (b) information that is due to be published;
   (c) information relating to the security services or the Royal household;
   (d) personal information or information provided to the authority in confidence;
   (e) information that is professionally privileged;
   (f) information that may prejudice the following:
      - national security, defence or the effectiveness of the armed forces;
      - international relations or relations between the administrations within the UK;
      - the country's economic interests;
      - criminal investigations or proceedings;
      - law enforcement;
      - the effective conduct of public affairs;
      - the physical or mental health of any individual; and
      - trade secrets or commercial interests.

7.2.3 Public Records and the Freedom of Information Act 2000

1. The Public Records Acts 1958 and 1967 provide access to public records at the Public Records Office after 30 years (the 30-year rule). Records can be kept closed for longer under s 5 of the 1958 Act or withheld if there is justification for so doing.
2. Under the Acts the Lord Chancellor has power to order release of documents sooner, if in the public interest.
3. Under the Freedom of Information Act a statutory regime

was created for access to public records, which replaced the provisions of the Public Records Act 1958 in respect of discretionary disclosure.

4. A recent review of the 30-year rule has been conducted and a report produced in January 2009. According to the report, the passing of the Freedom of Information Act has resulted in a great deal of information now being accessible long before it is 30 years old, particularly from central and local government, devolved administrations, and public bodies. In addition there are numerous official histories and unofficial memoirs published.

5. The report concludes the 30-year rule to be 'anachronistic and unsustainable' but that nevertheless some rule is required to ensure effective government. The recommendation in the report is to reduce the rule to 15 years.

7.2.4 Data Protection and the Freedom of Information Act

1. The Data Protection Act 1998 provides that personal data should be made available to individuals, primarily so that its accuracy may be checked.

2. Section 1 provides that you have the right to be informed if personal data is being held and to be told what that information is.

3. Data includes that held on both computer and in manual records.

4. Under ss 28 and 29 data may be withheld in the interests of national security, the prevention or detection of crime and the apprehension or prosecution of offenders.

5. The Act is regulated by a Data Protection Commissioner, who has the power to issue an enforcement notice on any data controller that fails to act in accordance with the Act.

6. The Freedom of Information Act extended the Data Protection Act in respect of access and data accuracy on information held by public authorities, and to personal data processed by or on behalf of Parliament.

CHAPTER 8

Membership of the European Community

Origins and development of the European Union
European Economic Community Treaty
Other Treaties
Single European Act; Treaty on European Union; Treaty of Amsterdam;
Treaty of Nice; Treaty Establishing a Constitution for Europe
Institutions
Council; Commission; European Parliament; European Court of Justice

Sources of EC law
Treaties; Regulations; Directives

The supremacy of EC law
Jurisprudence of the European Court of Justice
Van Gend en Loos; Costa; Internationale Handelsgesellschaft; Simmenthal

UK membership
European Communities Act 1972

Examining the obligation under s 2(4) ECA 1972
The 'rule of construction'
The primacy of EC law – the *Factortame* litigation

The impact on parliamentary supremacy
Changes to Dicey's doctrine – the removal of implied repeal;
Thoburn v Sunderland City Council (2002)
Retention of express repeal – *Macarthys* and *Garland*

8.1 The origins and development of European Community law

8.1.1 The Treaty of Rome 1957

1. The European Economic Community came into being with the Treaty of Rome, which established the foundations for a new level of European co-operation on issues of economic and social development. Initially there were six Member States. The UK joined in 1973 and at present there are 27 Member States.

2. The 27 Member States are:

Member State	Date of accession	Member State	Date of accession
Austria	1995	Latvia	2004
Belgium	1957	Lithuania	2004
Bulgaria	2007	Luxembourg	1957
Cyprus	2004	Malta	2004
Czech Republic	2004	Netherlands	1957
Denmark	1972	Poland	2004
Estonia	2004	Portugal	1985
Finland	1995	Romania	2007
France	1957	Spain	1985
Germany	1957	Slovakia	2004
Greece	1981	Slovenia	2004
Hungary	2004	Sweden	1995
Ireland	1972	United Kingdom	1973
Italy	1957		

8.1.2 Additional Treaties

1. The Single European Act, the Treaty on European Union (Maastricht Treaty), the Treaty of Amsterdam and the

Treaty of Nice provided for further integration in relation to economic, monetary and social policy.

2. The TEU further provides that the European Court of Justice must take account of the provisions of the European Convention on Human Rights (see Chapter 9) in its interpretation of EC law.

3. The Treaty Establishing a Constitution for Europe was signed in Rome in 2004. However, to come into effect each Treaty requires ratification in each of the Member States under their constitutional requirements. In some States this requires a positive vote in a national referendum – the French and Dutch no votes in 2005 suspended this Treaty.

4. The revised Treaty of Lisbon (or Reform Treaty) was signed in December 2007. The Treaty remains controversial. It was due to be ratified by the summer of 2008 but a 'no' vote in the Irish referendum has delayed this, although it has been ratified in the remaining 26 Member States. In Ireland the intention is to hold the referendum again in 2009 – a compromise reached between the Council and the Irish Government, part of which is agreement not to reduce the size of the Commission.

5. The main aims and objectives of the Community include (see Article 3/EC):
   - the establishment of a common market;
   - the abolition of measures obstructing the free movement of goods, persons, services and capital;
   - common policies relating to agriculture, fisheries, commerce and transport;
   - environmental protection;
   - strengthening consumer and health protection; and
   - forming associations with overseas countries to increase trade and jointly promote economic and social development.

8.2 The institutions

The following identifies, in brief, the main institutions of the European Union.

8.2.1 The Council of the European Union

1. The Council is attended by a government representative of each Member State who must be 'at ministerial level' and authorised to commit the Government of that Member State (Article 230/EC).
2. The Council is the principal decision-making body of the Union, where on most matters a decision is made by qualified majority voting on a weighted basis. Each State has a set number of votes based on its population size.

8.2.2 The Commission

1. Commissioners are appointed for a five-year term. The Commission represents the interest of the Union and must act in its best interests. Consequently, the Commissioners must act independently of their national Government (Article 213(2)/EC).
2. The Commission is the motive force behind Union policy and proposes policies and presents drafts of legislation to the Council.
3. The Commission is also the 'guardian' or 'watchdog' of the Treaties and ensures that the law is enforced and measures are implemented by the Member States. To this end it has the ability to enforce the law against a Member State in the European Court of Justice under Article 226/EC.

8.2.3 The European Parliament

1. Members of the European Parliament (MEPs) are elected by the citizens of the Member States every five years. The Parliament is therefore the only directly elected institution within the Community. However, the Parliament has no

direct law-making powers.

2. Over the years, though, the Parliament has seen a greater role in the decision-making process, with the introduction of new methods of creating legislation, such as co-decision and co-operation.

3. The Parliament also has the authority to dismiss the Commission; has some control over the Community's budget; and appoints an Ombudsman to receive complaints of maladministration by Union institutions (this does not extend to national institutions).

8.2.4 The European Court of Justice

1. The function of the Court is to ensure that in the interpretation and application of the Treaty the law is observed (Article 220/EC).

2. It hears cases brought by the institutions, Member States and individuals through the preliminary reference procedure under Article 234/EC.

3. Article 234 provides that domestic courts must refer questions of EC law to the Court where the national court is the final court of appeal in the case at hand. A lower court may refer such a question for a preliminary ruling/reference.

   - A preliminary ruling should be sought where the court cannot otherwise reach a decision on the issue, which itself must be central to the case (*Bulmer v Bollinger* (1974));

   - The purpose of Article 234 is to ensure uniform interpretation of EC law across all Member States (*CILFIT S & I v Ministro della Sanita* (1982)), a necessary prerequisite for the supremacy of Community law over national law.

4. The Court is assisted by a Court of First Instance, created by the Single European Act 1986. It currently has limited jurisdiction and hence does not hear preliminary references.

8.3 The sources of EC law

8.3.1 Treaties

1. Treaties form the primary source of EC law. The Treaties are directly applicable in that they are automatically incorporated into national law. In the UK this is achieved under s 2(1) of the European Communities Act 1972, which states that all Treaties are 'without further enactment to be given legal effect or used in the United Kingdom'.

2. In addition, the Treaties may have **direct effect**. This means that they are capable of creating rights that an individual may enforce in their own national courts.

3. In order to have direct effect, a provision must be clear and precise, unconditional and non-dependent, according to the case of *Van Gend en Loos* (1963).

4. Direct effect can be of two types. **Vertical** direct effect provides that the provision may be enforceable against the 'State', whereas **horizontal** direct effect provides that the provision may be enforced against another private or legal person. Treaty articles are capable of both types of direct effect.

8.3.2 Regulations

1. Regulations are a form of secondary legislation provided for under Article 249/EC. They are also binding without further enactment, known as **direct applicability**, which gives Regulations the effect of being 'binding in every respect' and automatically part of the legal system of every Member State (Article 249/EC). Member States must therefore enforce Regulations (*Commission v UK: Re Tachographs* (1979)).

2. Regulations, by their very nature, are capable of having both vertical and horizontal direct effect (*Leonesio v Ministero dell'Agricoltura* (1972)).

8.3.3 Directives

1. Directives are binding as to the result to be achieved by the implementing Member State. However, they require the State to choose the 'form and means' by which they will be implemented: Article 249/EC.
2. Directives are issued to Member States with a time limit for such implementation to occur.
   - If the Directive has not been implemented by the deadline, as long as it is clear and unconditional it may acquire vertical direct effect, according to the case of *Marshall v Southampton and South West Hampshire Area Health Authority* (1986).
   - Consequently, unimplemented Directives may be enforced only against the 'State', which has been broadly defined to include all decentralised government bodies as well as those bodies providing a public service under the control of the State (*Foster v British Gas* (1990)).
   - However, unimplemented Directives are not capable of having horizontal direct effect, which means that they cannot be relied on against a private body or an individual (*Marshall* and *Dori v Recreb Srl* (1994)).
3. Where a Directive has not been implemented, an individual who can satisfy the following test may be able to sue the State for damages suffered as a result of the non-implementation:
   - the Directive provides rights for individuals;
   - those rights are clearly defined in the Directive; and
   - there is a direct causal link between the failure to implement and the damage suffered (*Francovich and Bonifaci v Italian Republic* (1991) and *Dillenkoffer and Others v Federal Republic of Germany* (1996)).
4. If damage is caused by a Directive that has been incorrectly implemented, the breach must be 'manifest and serious' (*R v HM Treasury, ex parte BT plc* (1996)). This latter principle applies to all other breaches of Community law (*Brasserie du Pêcheur v Federal Republic of Germany*, joined

with *R v Secretary of State for Transport, ex parte Factortame* (1996)).

8.4 The supremacy of Community law

EC law was created as a supra-national legal system, which will prevail in the event of a conflict with a Member State's national law. This principle, along with that of direct effect (see above), was created by the European Court of Justice through its use of **teleological** or purposive interpretation of the EC Treaty.

- In *Van Gend en Loos* (1963) the ECJ stated that the 'Member States have limited their sovereign rights … and have created a body of law which binds both their nationals and themselves'.
- In *Costa v ENEL* (1964) there was conflict between a number of Treaty provisions and a later Italian law, which, under Italian constitutional law, would take priority. The ECJ held that it was impossible for a Member State to 'give preference to a unilateral and subsequent measure' and that precedence therefore had to be given to Community law.
- In *Internationale Handelsgesellschaft* (1970) the ECJ held that an EC Regulation took priority over the codified principles of the German constitution.
- In *Simmenthal SpA (No. 2)* (1979) the Court stated that national courts are under a duty to give full effect to the provisions of EC law and, if necessary, should refuse to apply national laws that conflict with EC law.

8.5 The European Communities Act 1972

By the enactment of the European Communities Act, the UK incorporated the legal system of the Community into English law.

Section	Content	Explanation
s 2(1)	Rights, liberties, obligations, restrictions, remedies, procedures … under the Treaties are without further enactment to be used, followed, enforced … in the UK	Treaty provisions shall be directly applied in English law
s 2(2)	Her Majesty may by Order in Council, and designated Ministers or Departments may by regulations, make provisions for the purpose of implementing Community obligations or enabling any rights to be enjoyed	The Government has power to implement provisions to give effect to Community law
s 2(4)	… any enactment passed or to be passed…shall be construed and have effect subject to the foregoing provisions …	The principle is retrospective; Acts passed before the ECA must be read as intending to conform to Community obligations. The **prospective** effect of this provision has caused considerable legal debate (see below)
s 3(1)	… any question as to the meaning and effect … of the Treaties or other Community instrument … shall be treated as a question of law …	The interpretation of rights and obligations is to be decided under Community law, by the ECJ or according to its principles or decisions

8.6 The European Communities Act 1972 and parliamentary supremacy

1. The effect of the ECA 1972 on the principle of parliamentary supremacy has been the focus of considerable legal and political debate. The main difficulty stems from s 2(4) of the Act, which provides that **future** legislation will also have to be compatible with Community law.

2. The difficulty in achieving this derives from the fundamental constitutional principle of **implied repeal**, discussed in detail in Chapter 4. In brief, implied repeal is the mechanism protecting the principle that no one Parliament can bind a successor Parliament. Consequently, no legislation can be entrenched and protected from future repeal, either expressly or by implication.

3. Reconciling the doctrine of parliamentary supremacy with that of Community law supremacy was therefore difficult. This is particularly so because the choice of national measure to bring effect to Community law was to introduce an ordinary statute – under the traditional doctrine of parliamentary supremacy, such an Act would itself be subject to implied repeal by any later legislation.

8.7 Judicial interpretation of s 2(4) ECA 1972

8.7.1 The rule of construction

1. The courts have taken two approaches to interpreting the obligation under s 2(4) of the Act.
   - In *Macarthys v Smith* (1979) the Court of Appeal concluded that the effect of the ECA was to require the court to undertake a process of **interpretation**. Thus, the national court will interpret the national law in the light of Community law to ensure that it complies;

- In *Garland v BREL* (1982) the House of Lords accepted this approach. Lord Diplock stated that English courts were well used to the concept of interpreting national law so that it conformed with Treaty obligations.
- In *Webb v EMO Air Cargo (UK) Ltd* (1992) the House of Lords confirmed that the courts are obligated to construe a statute so it complies with EC law (in this case a directive), regardless of whether the statute is passed before or after the EC law.

2. Examples of the use of this process of interpretation include:
   - In *Litster v Forth Dry Dock Ltd* (1990) the House of Lords interpreted a UK regulation, contrary to its clear meaning, in order to ensure its compatibility with an EC directive.
   - In *Pickstone v Freemans plc* (1989) the House of Lords departed from a literal interpretation of a statute so it could ensure compatibility with EC law.

3. This approach is sometimes referred to as the **'rule of construction'** and it acknowledges the supremacy of Community law, albeit through a 'back door' route. Indeed, the ECJ has concluded that all national courts are under an obligation to interpret national law in the light of the wording and purpose of Community law: *Von Colson and Kamann* (1984) and *Marleasing* (1990).

4. The rule of construction approach, however, is not sufficient to secure the full supremacy of Community law. What is required is the ability of a court to set aside statutes that conflict with Community law. However, the traditional concept of parliamentary supremacy would make this impossible, because of implied repeal and the enrolled Act rule, which provides that no body can question the authority of an Act of Parliament.
   - In *Felixstowe Dock and Railway Company v British Transport and Docks Board* (1976) Lord Denning concluded that all he would be able to do with an Act passed after 1972 would be to apply it, regardless of the

obligation set out in s 2(4) of the ECA 1972 or
Community law in general.

8.7.2 The *Factortame* litigation

1. The most significant development on the issue of
   compatibility came about in the *Factortame* litigation,
   arising from the conditions placed on the registration of
   Spanish vessels to fish within UK waters via the Merchant
   Shipping Act 1988.

   (a) The ECJ ruled in 1989 (*Case 213/89)* that the
       Merchant Shipping Act 1988 should be suspended
       since it was incompatible with a number of principles
       of Community law enshrined in the Treaty, such as
       the freedom of establishment and the prohibition of
       discrimination based on nationality. This was,
       however, ignored by the British Government.

   (b) In *R v Secretary of State for Transport, ex parte
       Factortame (No. 2)* (1989) the House of Lords
       granted interim relief to the applicants and disapplied
       the offending provisions of the Merchant Shipping
       Act. This only occurred after the European Court of
       Justice provided a preliminary reference. The
       reference focused on whether a constitutional
       principle had to be set aside to secure an individual's
       Community rights. The Court, following the
       judgment it had given in earlier cases (see above),
       stated that all principles of national law, regardless of
       status within the national system, had to be set aside
       in such circumstances. Lord Bridge concluded that 'it
       was the duty of a United Kingdom court, when
       delivering final judgment, to override any rule of
       national law to be found in conflict with any directly
       enforceable rule of Community law'.

   (c) In *R v Secretary of State for Transport, ex parte
       Factortame (No. 5)* (1999) the House of Lords ruled
       that the UK was sufficiently in breach of the

applicant's Community rights for the applicant to be awarded substantial damages. (See also *R v Secretary of State for Employment, ex parte EOC* (1995).)

8.8 The impact on the doctrine of parliamentary supremacy

1. As a result of judicial interpretation of the obligation stemming from s2(4) of the ECA 1972 (either by the rule of construction or by simply granting EC law primacy as in the *Factortame* litigation) we can conclude that there have been changes to the traditional doctrine of Parliamentary supremacy.

2. In particular, the constitutional principle of implied repeal has been **suspended** in relation to both:
   - the ECA 1972 itself, meaning that it is to some extent **entrenched** from change, thus binding a successive Parliament; and
   - to any legislation passed post-1972. In other words, all legislation passed since 1972 and in the future has to conform to EC law because of the obligation stemming from s 2(4). If a statute fails to conform to EC law the doctrine of implied repeal will not apply and the Act will be overridden by the EC legal principle.

3. This is now recognised by the courts, witnessed particularly in the judgement of *Thoburn v Sunderland City Council* (2002), by referring to the ECA 1972 as one of a range of **'constitutional statutes'**. According to the Court of Appeal in this case such statutes cannot be subject to implied repeal. (For further discussion see sections 2.1 and 4.5.)

4. However, it should be noted that this limitation on Parliament is one that it has placed on itself by virtue of passing the ECA 1972. Consequently, the courts have concluded that should Parliament ever **expressly** state that the provisions of a statute are to stand regardless of their

compatibility with Community law the courts will be bound to apply such a statute. This was the conclusion reached by both the Court of Appeal and the House of Lords in the cases of *Macarthys* and *Garland* (above).

5. To date, the above scenario has not occurred. It could be suggested that the political consequences of doing so would render the likelihood of such an event happening extremely unlikely.

CHAPTER 9

Human Rights and the Human Rights Act 1998

THE EUROPEAN CONVENTION ON HUMAN RIGHTS AND FUNDAMENTAL FREEDOMS

- Background, institutions and procedure
- Substantive Rights and Protocols
- Procedure
- Margin of Appreciation
- Derogation and Reservation
- Interpretation in the ECrtHR

Human Rights and the UK
Status of the ECHR pre 2000; *ex parte Brind* (1991)

Human Rights Act 1998

Section 3	The interpretative obligation
Section 4	Declarations of incompatibility; *R (Anderson) v Home Secretary* (2002)
Section 10	Fast-track procedure
Section 6	Public bodies; *Aston Cantlow* (2003); *Poplar Housing* (2001); *YL v Birmingham City Council* (2007)
Section 7	Standing
Section 8	Remedies

- Illustrative cases
- Impact of the HRA

9.1 The European Convention on Human Rights and Fundamental Freedoms

9.1.1 Background

1. The Council of Europe was founded in 1949 with the goal of post-war harmonisation across Europe. The Council accepted the United Nations' Declaration of Human Rights 1948 as a model for a European charter and the European Convention on Human Rights and Fundamental Freedoms came into force on 3rd December 1953.

2. The Convention established a European Court of Human Rights, which sits at Strasbourg. It may convene as a committee of three judges, as a chamber of seven, or in Grand Chamber of all 17 judges.

9.1.2 Procedure

1. Applications to the Court may be brought by States, an individual, groups of individuals and non-governmental organisations. The applicant must be personally affected by the issue.

2. Under Article 35 of the Convention, an applicant cannot proceed to the ECrtHR until all domestic remedies available are first exhausted. An application must be made within six months of the final decision of the highest court having jurisdiction.

9.1.3 The substantive rights and protocols

1. The substantive rights are identified in Articles 2–13 of the Convention:

Article	Right
2	**Right to life** Allowable exceptions excuse unintentional death as result of violent situations e.g. to quell riots, acting in self-defence but force used must be 'no more than absolutely necessary'
3	**Freedom from torture, inhuman and degrading treatment**
4	**Freedom from slavery and forced labour** Does not include compulsory labour as part of lawful detention
5	**Right to liberty and security of person** Applies except in accordance with lawful arrest or detention
6	**Right to a fair trial** before an independent and impartial tribunal • Protects the presumption of innocence • Provides for minimum rights to receive information and prepare defence • Special circumstances can be justified where publicity would prejudice national security or the interests of justice e.g. protection of juveniles
7	**Prohibition of retrospective criminal law**
8	**Respect for private and family life** Interference with this right by the State is permitted only if necessary in a democratic society including in the interests of: • National security; • Public safety; • Economic well-being of the State; • Prevention of disorder and crime; • Protection of health and morals; and • Protection of the rights and freedoms of others
9	**Freedom of thought, conscience and religion** Interference with this right by the State is permitted only if necessary in a democratic society including in the interests of: • Public safety; • Public health and morals; and • Protection of the rights and freedoms of others The protection of the right to privacy is limited
10	**Freedom of expression** Interference with this right by the State is permitted only if necessary in a democratic society including in the interests of: • National security; • Territorial integrity; • Public safety; • Prevention of disorder and crime;

	• Protection of health and morals; • Protection of the reputation or rights of others; and • Prevention of the disclosure of information received in confidence or to maintain the authority and impartiality of the judiciary
11	**Freedom of assembly and association** Interference with this right by the State is permitted only if necessary in a democratic society including in the interests of: • National security; • Public safety; • Prevention of disorder and crime; • Protection of health and morals; and • Protection of the rights and freedoms of others
12	**Freedom to marry and found a family** Rights must be exercised according to the State's laws on marriage
13	**Right to an effective remedy**

2. Article 14 does not provide a substantive right but that the rights and freedoms of the Convention are to be enjoyed by all, regardless of race, age, sex, language or other classification. A case cannot be founded purely upon Article 14; discrimination on the application of a substantive right must be shown.

3. In addition to the substantive rights set out in the Convention, there are a series of Protocols.

Protocol	Coverage
First	Article 1 – right to peaceful enjoyment of possessions Article 2 – education Article 3 – holding of regular and free elections
Fourth	Freedom of movement
Sixth	Abolition of the death penalty
Seventh	Appeals in criminal cases
Ninth	Procedural matters
Tenth	Minority rights

The UK is not party to the Fourth, Sixth or Seventh Protocols.

9.1.4 The margin of appreciation

1. While a State has positive obligations under the Convention, the European Commission and the Court recognise that there should be a degree of discretion permitted, on the basis that each State is uniquely placed to gauge the necessity for limitations on Convention rights within its territory.
2. If such measures are challenged, the Court will require the State to justify its actions and demonstrate their reasonableness.

9.1.5 Proportionality

1. The Convention itself makes reference to the need to uphold rights whilst ensuring that the community, the State and individuals are not thereby damaged.
2. The exercise of a right must therefore be proportionate to the effects of such exercise on others. Similarly, the response of the State to an administrative or legislative necessity must be proportionate to the desired outcome. For example, it would not be proportionate to tackle the smuggling of a particular lawful product by banning all imports of that product.

9.1.6 Derogation and reservation

1. Derogation by a State is not permitted in respect of all Convention rights. Only in specific circumstances (e.g. a state of emergency) can a State inform the Council of Europe that it will take steps that do not conform to its obligations. For example, in 2002 the UK entered a new derogation in respect of Article 5 in order to legitimise detention of non-nationals pending determination of their asylum status.
2. Reservations may be entered only before ratification. Under a reservation, the State will accept the obligations of a particular Convention right, subject to the application of its domestic legislation then in force.

9.1.7 Interpretation of the substantive rights in the European Court of Human Rights

Some illustrative examples of ECrtHR decisions on the scope of the substantive rights under the Convention in the context of the UK include:

Article 2	
Case	**Decision**
Paton v UK (1980)	Right to life begins at birth
McGann v UK (1996)	Lack of control over a covert military operation resulted in the 'more than was absolutely necessary' deaths of suspected terrorists
Pretty v UK (2001)	There is no right to assisted suicide
Evans v UK (2007)	The right to refuse an ex-partner the ability to use embryos does not violate Article 2 (or Article 8, see below)

Article 3	
Case	**Decision**
East African Asians v UK (1983)	Immigration controls based on racial discrimination amount to degrading treatment
D v UK (1997)	Deportation of an individual to a country lacking suitable health care that could result in their death violates the Article
Chahal v UK (1997)	A person cannot be forcibly returned to their country of origin when they are likely to face torture, inhuman or degrading treatment
A v Secretary of State for the Home Department (No. 2) (2005)	Evidence obtained by torture in another country cannot be used in the courts

Article 5	
Case	Decision
Johnson v UK (1996)	Failure to release a mentally ill patient because of lack of suitable accommodation breaches the Article
T and V v UK (1999)	Setting sentence periods without an opportunity for the lawfulness of the continued detention to be judicially reviewed breaches the Article
Murray v UK (1994)	The State must have 'reasonable suspicion' of an offence to justify detention
Caballero v UK (2000)	Automatic denial of bail for some offences breaches the Article
O'Hara v UK (2001)	Arrested persons must be brought before a judge in a prompt and timely manner

Article 6	
Case	Decision
Osman v UK (1999)	Striking out a negligence claim against the police on the grounds of public policy breached the Article
T and V v UK (1999)	Trying juveniles in an adult court violates the Article
Steel and Morris v UK (2005)	Denial of legal aid to defend a libel action brought by McDonalds breached the Article

Article 8	
Case	Decision
Dudgeon v UK (1982)	Prohibition under statute of homosexual acts between male adults in Northern Ireland amounted to a breach of the Article
Malone v UK (1984)	Tapping of a private telephone without a warrant breached the Article
McMichael v UK (1993)	If interference with family life is justified in the interests of a child the family member's rights must still be protected
Lustig-Praen and Beckett v UK (2000)	Banning homosexuals in the armed forces breached the Article

Article 10	
Case	**Decision**
Sunday Times v UK (1979)	The common law on contempt of court was too imprecise and unsatisfactory to justify the granting of an injunction and this was a breach of the Article. The UK changed the law by passing the Contempt of Court Act 1981
The Observer and The Guardian v UK (1991)	The continuation of injunctions against the publication of 'Spycatcher' had breached the Article because they were no longer justifiable since the information was no longer confidential
Goodwin v UK (1996)	A court order under the Contempt of Court Act 1981 to disclose a journalist's sources violated the Article

Article 12	
Case	**Decision**
Hamer v UK (1981)	Prohibiting prisoners from marrying breached the Article
Cossey v UK (1992)	The Article was not breached by prohibition of transsexual marriage

9.2 The status of the ECHR prior to the Human Rights Act 1998

1. The UK was an early signatory to the Convention and accepted the right to individual petition in 1965 but the UK courts were not bound to apply the Convention directly until incorporated into UK law by statute.
2. However, where there were two interpretations of national law, one in conformity with the Convention and one not, the courts would presume it was Parliament's intention to legislate in conformity: *R v Secretary of State for the Home Department, ex parte Brind* (1991).
3. The duty to interpret national law in light of the obligations under the Convention related to both legislation (*Waddington v Miah* (1974)) and the common law (*Derbyshire County Council v Times Newspapers Ltd* (1993)).

9.3 The Human Rights Act 1998

9.3.1 The Act

1. The Human Rights Act 1998 came into effect on 2nd October 2000.
2. The Act incorporates the ECHR into domestic law, making it directly enforceable in the UK courts. The Act gives 'further effect' to the Convention rights, which appear in Schedule 1. The Act does not give effect to Article 13 of the Convention (the right to an effective remedy).
3. Section 1 provides that Convention rights are to have effect subject to any reservation or derogation in force.

9.3.2 Section 3 – the interpretative obligation

1. Section 3 states that 'so far as it is possible to do so primary legislation and subordinate legislation must be read and given effect in a way which is compatible with the Convention rights'.
2. The courts have held that this requires **more** than ordinary statutory interpretation. If considered necessary the courts will read words into a statute to ensure compliance with the Convention: *R v A (Complainants' Sexual History)* (2002).
3. In *Ghaidan v Mendoza* (2004) the House of Lords held that even if the ordinary meaning of a statute is clear, a court may distort its language or read in additional words in order to achieve a meaning that is compatible with the Convention.
4. The courts are therefore required to take a **purposive** approach to the interpretation of legislation.
5. However, there should, because of the doctrine of parliamentary supremacy, be a distinction between legitimate interpretation and effectively undertaking the redrafting of legislation. This has been recognised by the courts:

- In *W and B (Children: Care Plan)* (2002) the House of Lords concluded that the Court of Appeal's interpretation of the Children Act 1989 could not be upheld;
- In *R v DPP, ex parte Kebeline and Others* (1999) Lord Hope referred to areas where the judiciary must defer to the 'considered opinion of the elected body' (see also *R v Lambert, Ali and Jordan* (2001)).

9.3.3 Section 4 – declarations of incompatibility

1. The Human Rights Act 1998, however, respects the doctrine of the supremacy of Parliament in that if there is a breach of the Convention the courts are not able to declare the Act invalid.
2. Instead the High Court and superior courts may make a **'declaration of incompatibility'** under s 4.
3. However, the power to issue a declaration of incompatibility only exists if there is a duty of interpretation under s 3 and that process has first been attempted.
4. A declaration of incompatibility cannot therefore be issued when the facts of a case took place before the Human Rights Act came into force: *Wilson v First County Trust (No. 2)* (2003). The Act consequently has no retrospective effect.
5. Section 4(6) provides that a declaration of incompatibility is not binding on the parties and does not affect the validity of legislation. The Government therefore has to decide whether it wishes to present to Parliament amendment or repeal of the offending legislation.
6. For example, in *R (Anderson) v Secretary of State for the Home Department* (2002) the House of Lords made a declaration of incompatibility in relation to the ability of the Home Secretary to decide the minimum period of incarceration for a murderer. It was concluded that this was a breach of Article 6 of the Convention – it did not

provide for a fair trial because such a decision was not being made by an independent and impartial tribunal but by a politician. The law was changed by the introduction of the Criminal Justice Act 2003.

7. A higher court may overturn a declaration of incompatibility made by a lower court on the grounds that there has in fact been no breach of the Convention. This occurred in, for example, *R (Alconbury Developments Ltd) v Secretary of State for the Environment, Transport and the Regions* (2001) and *Wilson v First County Trust (No. 2)* (2003).

9.3.4 Section 10 – the fast-track procedure

1. Where a declaration of incompatibility has been made, or a violation found, s 10 provides for a fast-track procedure to amend legislation.

2. The relevant Minister lays a draft order before Parliament for 60 days during which representation may be heard. Alternatively, the Minister may amend legislation by statutory instrument to remove the incompatibility where there are, in the Minister's opinion, compelling reasons for so doing.

3. For example, the fast-track procedure was used after the declaration of incompatibility issued in *R (H) v London North and East Mental Health Review Tribunal* (2001).

9.3.5 Section 6 – public authority

1. Section 6 makes it unlawful for a public authority to act in a way that is incompatible with Convention rights. 'Public authorities' includes courts and tribunals but neither Houses of Parliament.

2. To determine whether a body is a public authority reference can be made to the following factors (*Aston Cantlow and Wilmcote with Billesley Parochial Church Council v Wallbank* (2003)):
   - whether the body is publicly funded;

- whether the body is exercising statutory powers;
- whether the body is taking the place of central government or local authorities; and
- whether the body is providing a public service.

3. Examples of cases examining whether a body is a public authority include:
   - In *Aston Cantlow* (above) the Church Council was held not to be a public authority.
   - In *Poplar Housing and Regeneration Community Association Ltd v Donoghue* (2001) a housing association was held to be a public authority because it was exercising functions similar to a local authority.
   - In *YL v Birmingham City Council and Others* (2007) a privately owned, profit-making care home was held to not be a public authority.

9.3.6 Section 7 – standing

1. Section 7 provides that an individual may make an application only if they are the 'victim' of the alleged violation or, if not the immediate victim, are still affected.
2. Interest groups do not have standing to make an application unless they can establish that their members are or will be potential victims. However, interest groups that have expertise in the matter may be permitted by the court to make submissions.
3. The time limit for applications is one year from the alleged violation (s 7(5)) or within such period as the court considers equitable in the circumstances.

9.3.7 Section 8 – remedies

1. Section 8 provides for the court to award a remedy or 'make such order within its jurisdiction as it considers just and appropriate'.
2. Section 12(4) provides that in the case of an injunction application, the court is to have particular regard to the right of freedom of expression.

3. Damages are not awarded unless the court is satisfied they are necessary. In *Anufrijeva v London Borough of Southwark* (2003) the Court of Appeal concluded that damages should be considered a last resort under the Act. The scale of damages for any maladministration has to be modest.

9.3.8 Illustrative cases

- *R v Her Majesty's Advocate* (2000) – a nine-month delay between interview and charge of a suspect was held unreasonable and a violation of Article 6.
- *R v (Pretty) v DPP* (2001) – Article 2 did not extend to the right to die.
- *Douglas v Hello! Ltd* (2001) – Article 8 extended to the prevention of publication of materials in breach of confidence, although there was no duty of confidentiality in the case at hand. (It should be noted that the English courts have responded to Article 8 by deciding not to create a new tort of privacy but by developing the law of breach of confidence: see for example *Wainwright v Home Office* (2003)).
- *A v Secretary of State for the Home Department* (2002) – differential treatment between nationals and non-nationals in times of public emergency, in this case the threat of terrorism, was recognised under international law and was not a violation of the Convention.
- *R (Anderson) v Secretary of State for the Home Department* (2002) – the Home Secretary was not independent under Article 6 in terms of reviewing the detention of prisoners serving life sentences.
- *Attorney-General's Reference (No. 4 of 2002)* (2003) – reversal of the normal burden of proof so that an alleged terrorist had to prove they were not a terrorist under the Terrorism Act 2000 did not breach Articles 6 or 10.
- *R (KB) v Mental Health Review Tribunal* (2003) – patients' hearings had not been sufficiently speedy and they were therefore entitled to damages.

- *R (Ullah) v Special Adjudicator* (2004) – Article 3 of the Convention would be breached by a decision to expel an individual to a country where they would be likely to face torture, inhuman or degrading treatment.
- *R (Limbuela) v Secretary of State for the Home Department* (2005) – Article 3 may be breached if the State fails to provide the barest life necessities for asylum seekers.
- *R (Dudson) v Secretary of State for the Home Department* (2005) – Article 6 did not require oral hearings at every stage for criminal proceedings to be a fair and public hearing.
- *R (Begum) v Denbigh High School* (2006) – a school policy on permissible uniforms prohibiting the jilbab was not a breach of Article 9.
- *R (Baiai) v Secretary of State for the Home Department* (2007) – legislation requiring Home Office permission to marry if subject to immigration controls or an illegal immigrant breached Articles 12 and 14; each case would have to be examined on its merits.
- *Van Colle and Another v Chief Constable for Hertfordshire Constabulary* (2007) – failure by the police to adequately protect a prosecution witness was a violation of Articles 2 and 8.
- *R (Gentle) v PM* (2008) – Article 2 does not impose on the UK Government an obligation to ensure legality of its action prior to sending troops or to carry out a public enquiry into their deaths.

9.4 The impact of the Human Rights Act 1998

1. Declarations of incompatibility have not been common and even when made it has not been unusual for a higher court to overturn them.

2. Originally it appeared that the courts were prepared to create what Lord Steyn called a 'new legal landscape'. In *R v Lambert* (2001) Lord Slynn commented that the Human Rights Act had to be given its 'full import' and that 'long entrenched ideas may have to be put aside'.

3. However, later cases have shown that the courts have been rather more cautious, or conservative, in applying the Act.

4. The reasoning for such an approach can be seen in *R v DPP, ex parte Kebeline* (1999) where Lord Hope concluded that in certain areas the judiciary should defer 'on democratic grounds, to the considered opinion of the elected body or person whose act or decision is said to be incompatible with the Convention'. A similar approach can be seen in the decision of the House of Lords in *Bellinger v Bellinger* (2003).

5. The courts appear to prefer to exercise the interpretative power under section 3 of the Act than the power to issue a declaration of incompatibility under section 4. In *Ghaidan v Mendoza* (2004) Lord Steyn referred to section 3 as the 'lynch-pin' and section 4 as a 'measure of last resort'.

6. This is a reflection of the unwillingness of the courts to come into direct conflict with the executive.

7. It does not appear that the Act paves the way for the Convention to provide the basis from which the UK can develop it own version of protected human rights. In *R (S) v Chief Constable of South Yorkshire* (2004) the Court of Appeal suggested that English law develop its own higher standard of human rights. The House of Lords rejected this approach, stating that the application of the Convention should be decided on a uniform basis throughout the Member States.

8. However, in 2007 the PM announced the start of national consultation on the creation of a new Bill of Rights and Responsibilities for the United Kingdom.

CHAPTER 10

Freedom of the Person, Association and Assembly

FREEDOM OF THE PERSON

Article 5 ECHR

Police and Criminal Evidence Act 1984

- Powers of stop and search – safeguards
- Powers to search premises – safeguards
- Powers of arrest – section 24
- Powers of arrest – section 25
- Powers of arrest with a warrant
- Procedure on arrest – section 28
- Detention at the police station

Cases in the European Court of Human Rights

Blanket stop and search powers – Terrorism Act 2000

FREEDOM OF ASSOCIATION AND ASSEMBLY

Article 11 ECHR

Public Order Act 1986

- Offences
- Processions – sections 11–13
- Assemblies – section 14

Criminal Justice and Public Order Act 1994

Highways Act 1980

- *Hirst* (1986); *DPP v Jones* (1999)

Common law – breach of the peace

- *Bibby v CC of Essex* (2000); *Beatty v Gilbanks* (1882);
  Moss v McLachlan (1985)

Other legislation

10.1 Freedom of the person

10.1.1 Article 5 ECHR

1. Article 5 provides that everyone has the right to liberty and security. This Article is designed to protect individuals from arbitrary arrest and detention.
2. Article 5 further provides that a person may be deprived of their liberty in a limited number of circumstances and 'in accordance with a procedure prescribed by law'.
3. Detention is permitted:
   - following conviction by a competent court;
   - for non-compliance with a court order;
   - on reasonable suspicion of the suspect's having committed an offence;
   - to prevent the commission of an offence;
   - to prevent the escape of an offender;
   - to impose educational supervision upon a minor; and
   - pending deportation or to prevent unlawful entry into the State.
4. Article 5 provides for the right of a detained person to be informed promptly of the reasons for arrest and of the charges, in a language they understand. Article 5 further provides for the right to be brought promptly before a judicial authority.
5. A State may issue a notice of derogation, effectively suspending these provisions, in time of emergency under Article 15. Such derogation was in place with regard to Northern Ireland until the coming into force of the Terrorism Act 2000, for example.

10.1.2 The Police and Criminal Evidence Act 1984

1. The provisions regarding lawful arrest and detention are found in the Police and Criminal Evidence Act 1984 (PACE).

2. **Powers of stop and search are as follows:**
   - a police constable may stop and search people and vehicles in a place to which the public has access (s 1 PACE 1984);
   - a place to which the public has access includes a place where they have paid for entry; it also includes a garden or yard of private property where the constable has reasonable grounds for believing the person does not reside there and has not got the permission of the resident to be there;
   - in order to stop a vehicle the constable must be in uniform (s 2(9)(b) PACE);
   - in order to search a person or vehicle the constable must have **reasonable grounds** for suspecting that he will find stolen or prohibited articles (s 1(3) PACE);
   - police officers also have specific powers to stop and search under other legislation such as the Misuse of Drugs Act 1971, the Criminal Justice and Public Order Act 1994 (s 60), and the Terrorism Act 2000 (ss 44-45). Under the latter the police have the power to search any pedestrian or vehicle on the street. There is no need for any suspicion of an offence or any warrant: *R (Gillan) v Commissioner of Police for the Metropolis* (2003).

3. **Safeguards on the above powers are as follows:**
   - if a constable is not in uniform then he must produce documentary evidence that he is a police officer;
   - in all cases, before commencing the search, the constable must state his name and station to the suspect and specify the object of the proposed search and the grounds. If this is not done then the search is unlawful (*Osman v DPP* (1999));
   - if the search is in public, the constable can only request the removal of an outer coat, jacket and gloves (s 2(9)(a) PACE);
   - Code of Practice A gives the police guidance on the use of stop and search powers. In particular, it points out that reasonable suspicion can never be supported on the

basis of personal factors alone. Factors such as age, colour, hairstyle, manner of dress or known previous convictions cannot be used as the sole basis on which to search.

4. **Powers to search premises are as follows:**

   (a) a search warrant can be issued by a magistrate, allowing police to search premises named in the warrant. Such a warrant will only be issued where there are reasonable grounds for believing that:

   - a serious arrestable offence has been committed;
   - that there is material on the premises which is likely to be of substantial value to the investigation of the offence; and
   - that it is not practicable to communicate with any person entitled to grant entry to the premises or the material; OR entry to the premises will not be granted unless a warrant is issued; OR the purpose of the search may be frustrated or seriously prejudiced unless a constable arriving at the premises can gain immediate entry (s 8 PACE);

   (b) a search warrant must specify the premises to be searched and, as far as possible, the article sought;

   (c) a warrant only authorises one entry within one month from the date it is issued (s 16(3) PACE);

   (d) police may enter without a search warrant to arrest a person (on a warrant) or for an arrestable offence or to recapture an escaped prisoner (s 17 PACE);

   (e) if a person is arrested, the police can enter and search premises that were occupied or controlled by them (s 18 PACE);

   (f) if a person is arrested, the police can enter and search the premises that person was in at the time of the arrest or immediately beforehand (s 32 PACE);

   (g) there is a common law right to enter premises to prevent or deal with a breach of the peace. This right exists even though the breach of the peace is on private property (*McLeod v Commissioner of Police of the Metropolis* (1994));

(h) the police may enter and search any premises where the occupier consents.

5. **Safeguards on powers to search premises are as follows:**
   - where a warrant has been issued, the police are required to enter and search at a reasonable time unless the purpose of the search may be frustrated (s 16(4) PACE and Code of Practice B);
   - the police must identify themselves to the occupier, show the search warrant and provide a copy (s 16(5) PACE). This must be done at the time the search commences (*R v Longman* (1988));
   - sections 17 and 18 require the police to give anyone present in the premises the reason for entry. If this is not provided, the entry is unlawful (*O'Loughlin v Chief Constable of Essex* (1988));
   - the police can only exercise powers to enter and search under s 32 immediately after arrest (*R v Badham* (1987)).

6. **Powers of arrest under section 24 PACE:**
   - powers under s 24 PACE only operate where there is or may be an arrestable offence, which is any offence for which the sentence is fixed by law or the maximum sentence is at least five years and any other offence specifically made an arrestable offence;
   - any person may arrest someone in the act of committing an arrestable offence; someone whom they have reasonable suspicion of committing such an offence; someone guilty of committing an arrestable offence; and someone whom they have reasonable suspicion of being guilty of committing such an offence;
   - the police have additional powers to arrest where they have reasonable grounds for suspecting that an arrestable offence has been committed; where someone is about to commit an arrestable offence; and where they have reasonable grounds for suspecting someone is about to commit an arrestable offence.

7. **Powers of arrest under section 25 PACE:**
   - the police have power to arrest under general conditions where the suspect's name and address cannot be discovered or there are reasonable grounds for believing that those provided are false;
   - section 25 also allows police to arrest where there are reasonable grounds for believing that arrest is necessary to prevent that person from causing physical injury to themselves or any other person; causing loss or damage to property; committing an offence against public decency; causing an unlawful obstruction of the highway; or if there are reasonable grounds for believing that arrest is necessary to protect a child or other vulnerable person.

8. **Powers of arrest with a warrant:**
   - An application for a warrant for arrest may be made under s 1 Magistrates' Court Act 1980.
   - The application must be supported by written information and sworn oral evidence showing that the person has committed or is suspected of committing an offence punishable by imprisonment.
   - The warrant must name the person to be arrested.

9. **Other powers of arrest**
   - There are additional statutory powers to make an arrest, such as when a person granted police bail fails to attend the police station on the set date (s 46A PACE).
   - There is also a common law power to arrest for breach of the peace.

10. **Procedure on arrest:**
   - Section 28 PACE requires that, for the arrest to be lawful, the reasons must be given either at the time or at some more practicable time. A lawful arrest also requires the person to be informed of the fact of arrest.
   - According to *Taylor v Thames Valley Chief Constable* (2004) the arrested person must be informed in 'simple, non-technical language' that they can understand of both the legal and factual grounds for the arrest. An

officer is however not required to provide 'detailed particulars'.

- Where necessary, reasonable force may be used (s 117 PACE).
- Any warrant must be shown on demand or as soon as is reasonably practicable.
- The police may search the person for anything that may be used to make an escape or for evidence relating to the offence.
- If the search takes place in public, the suspect may be asked to remove only their outer coat, jacket and/or gloves.
- If the arrest is not made at a police station, the suspect must be taken to one as soon as practicable (s 30(1) PACE), although there may be a delay if it is necessary to carry out certain investigations immediately and the presence of the suspect is necessary in order to carry out those investigations (s 30(10) PACE).
- The reasons for any delay must be recorded on arrival at the police station (s 30(11) PACE).

11. Detentions at the police station:

- Once arrested, a person may be detained at the police station for questioning before being charged or released.
- A person may be detained for a maximum period of 36 hours for an indictable offence.
- The time period begins from the time of arrest, unless the person is arrested outside the relevant police area in which case the period runs from the time they arrive at the police station.
- The time period can be extended. If authorised by a senior police officer the period can be extended on the grounds that they reasonably believe (s 42 PACE):
  - the detention is necessary to secure/preserve evidence or obtain evidence by questioning;
  - the offence is indictable; and
  - the investigation is being conducted 'diligently and expeditiously'.

- Detention must be reviewed after 24 hours (s 42(4) PACE).
- ss 43–44 PACE, as amended by the Serious Organised Crime and Police Act 2005, provides that the police can apply to the Magistrates Court for a further extension of the time period of detention up to a possible maximum of 96 hours.
- At the beginning of the detention period, the custody officer must inform the suspect of their rights to have someone informed; to legal advice in private and free of charge; to consult the Codes of Practice; and to speak on the telephone for a reasonable period of time to one person.
- In the case of a serious arrestable offence, where it is believed that it will hinder the investigation, the right to have someone informed and the right to legal advice may be delayed for up to 36 hours.
- Where the suspect is under 17, a parent or guardian should be notified of the detention (s 34(2) Children and Young Persons Act 1933).
- The custody officer is responsible for reviewing the detention and deciding whether the person should continue to be detained. This must be done at the outset of the detention, after six hours, and every nine hours thereafter (s 40 PACE).
- A record of all events (such as visits to the cell and interviews) must be made by the custody officer.
- At the start of any interview, a suspect must be cautioned. However, the Criminal Justice and Public Order Act 1994 has eroded the right to silence by allowing adverse inferences to be made at trial where the accused failed at interview to mention facts or to account for objects, substances or remarks, or for their presence at a particular place.
- All interviews must be tape recorded (s 60 PACE).
- Suspects are entitled to have a lawyer present, except where the right to legal advice has been delayed under s 58 PACE.

- Suspects under 17 or those who are mentally disordered or disabled must have an appropriate adult present, even if they appear to understand the questions (*R v Aspinall* (1999)).
- There should be a short break at least every two hours, breaks for meals, and an eight-hour period of rest.
- Code of Practice E sets out rules and guidelines for the conduct of interviews.
- If a confession is obtained by oppression or in circumstances likely to render it unreliable, it can be excluded by the trial judge (ss 76 and 78 PACE).

10.1.3 Cases in the European Court of Human Rights

The following are some examples of cases heard by the European Court of Human Rights in the context of police powers.

- *Brogan and Others v UK* (1988) – the Court found no violation of Article 5 where the police had questioned individuals about specific offences and later released them, as 'reasonable suspicion' did not mean that the commission of the offence had to be established before arrest.
- *Fox, Campbell and Hartley v UK* (1990) – the Court found that reasonableness of suspicion with regard to terrorist offences may be judged to a different standard than that of other offences.
- *Steel v UK* (1998) – the Court found that the common law offence of breach of the peace was sufficiently clear to permit a lawful arrest in anticipation of such a breach.
- *Price v UK* (2001) – the conditions of detention in both a police station and prison for a severely disabled person violated Article 3 (freedom from inhuman and degrading treatment).
- *Edwards v UK* (2002) – the Court examined the murder of a prisoner killed by an inmate with a history of

violent, schizophrenic behaviour. It found violations of Article 2 (right to life), Article 1 (no effective investigation) and Article 13 (no effective remedy because the victim's parents could not secure compensation).

10.1.4 Blanket stop and search powers

1. Under ss 44-47 of the Terrorism Act 2000, blanket stop and search powers can be operated by the police. They must be authorised by a senior police officer and apply to a specific area. They can cover both vehicle and pedestrian stop and search.

2. Section 44(3) provides that authorisation can be granted if 'expedient for the prevention of acts of terrorism'.

3. Authorisation areas can be large; for example, the whole of London has been covered.

4. Authorisations must be approved by the Secretary of State within 48 hours of being made or they will cease to be effective. They apply for a maximum period of 28 days, unless renewed under s 46(7). Thus authorisations may be continually renewed.

5. If a person fails to stop in such an area or wilfully obstructs a police officer exercising these powers, they are liable to a fine of £5,000, a prison sentence of six months, or both (s 47).

6. The stop and search powers are **not** dependent on reasonable suspicion (s 45); they can only be exercised for the purpose of searching for articles that could be used in connection with terrorism. This is also repeated in Code A. However, breach of the Code does not render the search unlawful.

7. In *R (Gillan) v Commissioner of Police for the Metropolis* (2006) the two applicants were stopped and searched under s 44 of the Terrorism Act 2000 at a protest against an arms fair in London; neither search lasted for longer than 20 minutes. They argued that the stops and searches were in

breach of Article 5 ECHR. The House of Lords held that there had been no deprivation of liberty contrary to the Article.

8. It therefore seems that the blanket stop and search powers under the Terrorism Act 2000 can be potentially used against groups such as protesters. In addition, there are suggestions that they may be used in a racially motivated manner, in that ethnicity may be a criterion in deciding to exercise the powers: see *R (European Roma Rights Centre) v Immigration Officer at Prague Airport (UN High Commissioner for Refugees Intervening)* (2005).

10.2 Freedom of association and assembly

10.2.1 Article 11 ECHR

1. Article 11, paragraph 1, provides the right to freedom of peaceful assembly and to freedom of association with others.
2. Article 11, paragraph 2, permits lawful restrictions on this right by the armed forces, the police and the administration of the State.
3. Such restrictions must be 'necessary in a democratic society' and in the interests of:
   - national security or public safety;
   - prevention of disorder and crime;
   - protection of health and morals; or
   - protection of the rights and freedoms of others.

10.2.2 The Public Order Act 1986 offences

The Public Order Act 1986 contains provisions to restrain violent conduct in a public place. It has five principal offences:

Section 1 (riot)	Use or threat of unlawful violence	12 or more persons with a common purpose	Causes person of reasonable firmness to fear for their safety
Section 2 (violent disorder)	Use or threat of unlawful violence	3 persons	Causes person of reasonable firmness to fear for their safety
Section 3 (affray)	Use or threat of unlawful violence towards another	1 person	Causes person of reasonable firmness to fear for their safety
Section 4 (fear or provocation of violence)	Use of threatening, abusive, insulting words or behaviour or display of such towards another	1 person	Causes a specific person to believe immediate unlawful violence will be used
Section 5 (harassment, alarm or distress)	Use of threatening, abusive, insulting words or behaviour or display of such	1 person	Takes place within hearing or sight of a person likely to be caused harassment, alarm or distress

10.2.3 Assemblies and processions

1. Section 16 POA 1986 defines a public assembly as an 'assembly of 20 or more persons in a public place which is wholly or partly open to the air'.
2. The definition of a 'procession' comes from *Flockhart v Robinson* (1950): 'a body of persons moving along a route'.
3. *DPP v Jones* (1999) held that people demonstrating on a grass verge between Stonehenge and the A344 road were not guilty of trespassory assembly, as a peaceful assembly constituted a reasonable use of the highway as long as the right of passage was not impeded.
4. The following tables summarise the relevant legal provisions of the Public Order Act in relation to various activities connected with processions and assemblies.

Note: Demonstrations in a designated area around Parliament must be notified and the authorisation of the Metropolitan Commissioner obtained (ss 132–138 Serious and Organised Crime and Police Act 2005). The draft Constitutional Renewal Bill proposes to repeal these provisions.

Processions

Section	Activity	Regulations	Conditions	Offence
s 11	Processions to express views, campaign, gain publicity, commemorate	6 days' notice to be given to police	Spontaneous processions permitted	Offence to fail to notify or to alter procession route after publication
s 12	Processions	Prior conditions may be imposed to prevent serious public disorder, property damage, community disruption	Conditions may be imposed by a senior officer at the scene	Offence to fail to comply with conditions
s 13	Processions as above	Banning order may be made for up to 3 months if conditions insufficient	Requires consent of the local authority	Offence to organise or participate in a banned procession

Assemblies

Section	Activity	Regulations	Offence
s 14	Assembly	Conditions may be imposed on assemblies on s 12 grounds	Offence to fail to comply with conditions
s 14A	Assembly	Chief police officer may apply a banning order if the assembly is likely to ● involve trespass; ● seriously disrupt the community; ● cause damage to buildings or structures.	Offence to attend or organise a banned trespassory assembly
s 14C	Assembly	Police may stop persons within 5-mile radius of an assembly, subject to a s 14A order	Offence to fail to comply with direction to leave the area

10.2.4 The Criminal Justice and Public Order Act 1994

The CJPOA 1994 Part V provides a range of powers to remove travellers, including gypsies, hunt saboteurs and ravers, together with all vehicles, from public or private land.

	Activity	Conditions and powers	Offences
s 61	Trespassers present with the common purpose of residing on land	Persons and vehicles may be directed to leave by the senior police officer present if reasonable steps have been taken to ask them to leave; trespassers have caused damage or have been threatening or abusive; trespassers have 6 or more vehicles	Offence to fail to leave as soon as reasonably practicable or to return within 3 months
s 63	A gathering of 100 or more persons at a rave where loud music is likely to cause distress to locals	● 2 or more persons making preparations; ● 10 or more persons waiting for event to begin; ● 10 or more persons attending the event may be ordered by a superintendent to leave	An arrestable offence to fail to leave as soon as reasonably practicable
s 65	Persons on their way to a rave that has been stopped under s 63	Uniformed officer may stop persons and direct them not to proceed within 5 miles of rave	An arrestable offence to fail to obey the direction
s 69	Persons committing aggravated trespass by interfering with a lawful activity engaged in by others	The senior police officer present may direct a person suspected of aggravated trespass to leave	Trespass involving intimidation or obstruction of lawful activity and failing to leave when directed are arrestable offences
s 70	Trespassory assemblies	Chief police officer may apply for banning order	This section is activated under s 14A POA 1986 (see above)

10.2.5 The Highways Act 1980

1. Section 173 of the Highways Act 1980 makes it an offence wilfully to obstruct free passage along the highway without lawful authority or excuse.
2. Cases on the offence have considered the question of whether the holding of an assembly or the activities of speakers or protestors amount to a lawful use of the highway, which is not a public nuisance:
   - *Hirst v Chief Constable for West Yorkshire* (1986) – animal rights protestors' convictions were overturned on appeal because their actions outside a fur shop were sufficiently reasonable, given the need to recognise a right to demonstrate.
   - In *DPP v Jones* (1999) the House of Lords stated that it could be lawful to use the highway for the purposes of demonstrating. It is a matter of fact in each case as to whether that use is reasonable.

10.2.6 Common law – breach of the peace

1. The police have a **common law duty** to act to prevent a breach of the peace and it is within the discretion of the officer present whether and when it is reasonable to intervene in the proceedings for this purpose.
2. In *Bibby v Chief Constable of Essex* (2000) a breach of the peace was defined as an unreasonable 'sufficiently real and present threat' coming from the person to be arrested and which clearly interferes with the rights of others.
3. In *R (Laporte) v Gloucestershire Chief Constable* (2006) it was held that the common law power to prevent a breach of the peace is confined to a situation where the breach is actually taking place or is imminent. In this case the police were considered to have acted disproportionately in that the freedom of expression should only be limited as a last resort.

4. In contrast, in *Moss v McLachlan* (1985) the stopping of miners four miles from their intended destination at a picket line was held to be lawful because the police officer 'honestly and reasonably' formed the opinion that a breach of the peace was highly likely.

10.3 Other legislation

1. The Public Processions (Northern Ireland) Act 1998 provides for a Parades Commission to consider applications for processions in the special circumstances prevailing in the province.
2. The Police Act 1996 (s 89) makes it an offence to obstruct or assault the police in the execution of their duty.
3. Section 1 of the Public Order Act 1936 makes it an offence to wear a uniform signifying political affiliation and bans paramilitary training.
4. The Terrorism Act 2000 makes it an offence to be a member of or to support an organisation that is proscribed under Schedule 2 of that Act.
5. The Crime and Disorder Act 1998 provides for the granting of Anti-social Behaviour Orders (ASBOs) by Magistrates' and Country Courts. An ASBO prohibits the individual from doing anything identified in the order. The ASBO applies for a minimum period of two years and extends until the end of the period specified within the Order.

CHAPTER 11

Judicial Review: Jurisdiction, Procedure and Remedies

Defining the role of judicial review
- supervisory jurisdiction
- exclusivity principle

Judicial review and the Human Rights Act

Defining public bodies and public authorities

Limitations to judicial review
- justiciability
- exclusion clauses
- availability of alternative remedies

Procedural requirements
Supreme Court Act 1981
Civil Procedure Rules Pt 54 1998

Leave

Time limits

Sufficient interest
- personal individual sufficient interest
- in the interests of society as a whole
- pressure/ interest groups
- claims under the Human Rights Act 1998

Remedies

11.1 Defining the role of judicial review

1. Judicial review is the process whereby the judiciary examines the legality of the actions of the executive. Hence it represents the means by which the courts may control the exercise of governmental power.

2. Judicial review is closely aligned with securing the rule of law (see Chapter 3). For example:
   - Lord Hoffman in *R (Alconbury) v Secretary of State for the Environment, Transport and the Regions* (2001) described the significance of judicial review in terms of the constitution in the following terms: 'The principles of judicial review give effect to the rule of law. They ensure that administrative decisions will be taken rationally in accordance with a fair procedure and within the powers conferred by Parliament'.
   - Wade describes judicial review as 'an essential process if the rule of law is to be observed in a modern democracy'.

3. Judicial review is not an appeals process. In finding that a public body has exceeded its lawful authority, the court will not enquire into the subjective correctness of the decision, but only into the process by which the decision was reached. Unlike in an appeal, the court will therefore not substitute its own assessment of the merits.

4. The process of judicial review is therefore procedural in nature and determines whether a public body has acted within its powers (*intra vires*) or outside of its powers (*ultra vires*). If a body is determined to have acted *intra vires* its decision is not open to challenge under the process of judicial review.

5. Judicial review can consequently be described as a **supervisory**, rather than an appellate, jurisdiction.

6. Judicial review cannot be used for private law matters (see below). Where the matter is one of public law, judicial review must be used: *O'Reilly v Mackman* (1983). This is

known as the 'exclusivity principle'. However, where there is a combination of private and public law matters the courts may be willing to generate exceptions to the exclusivity principle: see for example *Roy v Kensington and Chelsea Family Practitioner Committee* (1992); *Mercury Communications Ltd v Director-General of Telecommunications* (1996); and *Clark v University of Lincolnshire and Humberside* (2000).

7. Cases are brought by the Crown on behalf of the applicant against a defendant public body.

11.2 Judicial review and the Human Rights Act 1998

1. The Human Rights Act 1998 has had a significant impact on judicial review. Public bodies have a legal duty to act in accordance with Convention rights; failure to do so may result in judicial review proceedings.

2. The application of judicial review under the Act differs from traditional judicial review in a number of ways including:
   - the interpretation of a public body; and
   - the standing or sufficient interest required to apply for judicial review.

   These aspects will be discussed further below.

3. In addition, judicial review on human rights claims may result in a 'declaration of incompatibility', which could result in reform of the law (see section 9.3).

4. The Human Rights Act also supplements the traditional judicial review requirements of natural justice by incorporating Article 6 of the ECHR in respect of the right to a fair trial (see Chapter 12).

11.3 Defining a public body

1. Judicial review is only available to challenge decisions made by public bodies. If the body is a private body, private law must be used.

2. There is no single test to identify a public body and the courts will examine a number of factors.
   - If a body is set up under statute or by delegated legislation then the source of its power means it is a public body and subject to judicial review.
   - However, where the matter is unclear, the courts should examine the 'nature of the power' being exercised. In *R v City Panel on Takeovers and Mergers, ex parte Datafin Ltd* (1987) it was held that if the body is exercising public law functions or if the exercise of its functions have public law consequences, it may be a public body and subject to judicial review.

3. Conversely, a body holding extensive regulatory powers may be concluded to be a private body, on the basis that such powers are based exclusively on contract or some other agreement to submit to their jurisdiction, for example disciplinary powers exercised by sporting or professional bodies: *R v Jockey Club, ex parte Aga Khan* (1993) and *R v Football Association, ex parte Football League* (1993).

4. Under the Human Rights Act 1998 challenge through the process of judicial review can be made against decisions of **public authorities**, defined under s 6 to include courts and tribunals and 'any person whose functions are functions of a public nature'. However, definition of a public authority within the context of the Human Rights Act has been narrowly interpreted (see for example *R (Julian West) v Lloyd's of London* (2004)).

5. To determine whether a body is a public authority reference can be made to the following factors (*Aston Cantlow and Wilmcote with Billesley Parochial Church Council v Wallbank* (2003)):

- whether the body is publicly funded;
- whether the body is exercising statutory powers;
- whether the body is taking the place of central government or local authorities; and
- whether the body is providing a public service.

(For further discussion see Chapter 9.)

11.4 Limitations to judicial review

11.4.1 Justiciability

1. The subject-matter must be suitable for review by the courts. If the matter is one of 'high policy' including national security, it may be considered by the courts as being non-justicable and therefore not amenable to the process of judicial review.

2. Matters of public high policy are determined by the executive and not the courts: *Nottinghamshire County Council v Secretary of State for the Environment* (1986) and *R v Parliamentary Commissioner for Administration, ex parte Dyer* (1994).

3. The courts will also be cautious in examining exercises of the royal prerogative particularly where issues of national security are involved: *Council for Civil Service Unions v Minister for the Civil Service* (1985).

4. For example, the courts will not consider whether the executive's prerogative of treaty-making has been exercised unlawfully: *R v Secretary of State for Foreign and Commonwealth Affairs, ex parte Rees-Mogg* (1994). The courts will also not review the content of a treaty: *Blackburn v Attorney-General* (1971).

5. However, in more recent times the courts have shown an increased willingness to examine exercises of prerogative powers (see Chapter 6).

11.4.2 Exclusion of judicial review

1. Statute has been used to attempt to limit the availability of judicial review in two main ways.

2. **Complete (or finality) ouster clauses** provide that the decision made by the public body is final and hence not subject to any review.

3. The leading case on such clauses is *Anisminic v Foreign Compensation Commission* (1969). According to this case a court may conclude that judicial review is available regardless of the clause on the basis that the decision itself was not within the powers conferred. In other words it was *ultra vires* and not a decision at all, therefore it fell outside of the ouster clause. It would not be the intention of Parliament to remove the jurisdiction of the courts to judicially review such decisions.

4. In *R v Medical Appeal Tribunal, ex parte Gilmore* (1957) a statutory provision stating that any decision of the Tribunal was final was held to mean that whilst the decision could not be re-opened by the Tribunal and no other right to appeal could apply, it did not prevent the decision being subject to the supervisory jurisdiction of judicial review.

5. However, certain clauses may be upheld as preventing judicial review if they are precisely drafted and still provide for some review of the decision. One example of this is a **time limit clause**.

6. These provide that judicial review can only be applied for within a defined and often short period of time and that thereafter the decision shall not be questioned in a court of law (for example, statutes relating to planning and compulsory purchase orders).

7. Such clauses are justified on the basis of the need to ensure particular matters are not delayed or impeded in implementation.

8. These clauses are generally upheld by the courts. For example, in *R v Cornwall CC, ex parte Huntingdon* (1994)

it was concluded that the clause was valid on the basis that it did not completely exclude any possibility of review of the decision and was necessary to meet the purpose of the statute, namely to ensure quick development of the land in question: see also *R v Secretary of State for the Environment, ex parte Ostler* (1976).

11.4.3 Availability of alternative remedies

1. In deciding whether to grant leave (see below) the court may also take into account whether alternative remedies are available: *R v Inland Revenue Commissioners, ex parte Preston* (1985).
2. For example, if there are statutory rights of appeal these should be exhausted prior to any action for judicial review: *R v Secretary of State for the Home Department, ex parte Swati* (1986).
3. Generally, the court will exercise its discretion and, if an alternative appeals process is considered satisfactory, will decline to grant leave for judicial review (*Leech v Deputy Governor of Parkhurst Prison* (1988)) unless there are exceptional circumstances (*R (Sivasubramanian) v Wandsworth County Court* (2003)).

11.5 Procedural requirements

1. The basis for judicial review is found in the:
   - **Supreme Court Act 1981**; and
   - **Civil Procedure Rules Pt 54 1998** which came into effect in 2000.

   These set out a number of procedural requirements.
2. Claims for judicial review are made to the Administrative Court and have two main stages:
   - the request for leave; and
   - the substantive hearing.
3. Prior to the request for leave there is pre-action protocol that the applicant should write to the body identifying the

issues and that the body reply. This is not obligatory. Because this process can ensure a settlement, thereby removing the need for litigation, the court will usually expect the parties to comply with it. The procedural requirements are then as follows.

11.5.1 Leave

1. The Supreme Court Act 1981 section 31 states that 'no application for judicial review shall be made unless the leave of the High Court has been obtained'.
2. The requirement of **leave**, or permission, acts as a filter to remove unmeritorious claims.
3. Judicial review is therefore not available as a right since it is discretionary on the acceptance of the court.
4. Leave was previously sought *ex parte* (without the other side) but it is now *inter partes* so the court is aware of both sides of the argument.
5. This part of the process is mostly based on written submissions, though the court may convene an oral hearing.

11.5.2 Time limits

1. Under the Civil Procedure Rules 1998 rule 54.5, an action (completion of the claim form) must be brought 'promptly' and in any event no later than **three months** after the grounds to make the claim first arose (r 54.5(1)(b)).
2. This may be reduced by statute in specific areas (see above). Conversely, it may also be extended by the court at its discretion.

11.5.3 Sufficient interest

1. Section 31 of the Supreme Court Act 1981 provides that 'the court shall not grant leave ... unless it considers that the applicant has a sufficient interest in the matter to which the application relates'. Sufficient interest is also

known as *locus standi* or standing.

2. **Sufficient interest** will be assessed by the court at both the leave stage and at the substantive hearing: *R v Inland Revenue Commissioners, ex parte National Federation of Self-employed and Small Businesses* (1982).

3. The need for sufficient interest prevents what Lord Scarman described in the above case as 'abuse by busybodies, cranks and other mischief makers'. It therefore ensures cases are genuine and avoids unnecessary interference with administrative decisions and processes.

4. Applicants for judicial review are generally of four types:
   - individuals whose personal rights and interests are affected by a decision;
   - individuals concerned that a decision has affected the interests of society as a whole;
   - pressure or interest groups who believe a decision affects the rights or interests of their members or society as a whole; and
   - individuals claiming for judicial review for a breach of human rights under the Human Rights Act 1998.

a) Individual personal sufficient interest

1. This will depend on the facts of the case and is determined by the court exercising its discretion. It will be relatively easy to establish sufficient interest if the individual is directly or indirectly affected by the decision. There will, for example, be clear indication of sufficient interest if a person's property or livelihood will be affected.

2. Some examples of personal individual sufficient interest include:
   - an individual being excluded the right to enter the country (*Schmidt v Secretary of State for Home Affairs* (1969)); and
   - a gypsy trying to ensure their local authority provided an adequate site for them as required by statute (*R v Secretary of State for the Environment, ex parte Ward* (1984)).

b) Individuals representing the interests of society as a whole

1. In some cases an individual may be granted sufficient interest because they are representing the public interest in a matter.

2. Some examples of sufficient interest in this context include:
   - an individual concerned with the budget of the EU, on the basis that the person was a taxpayer (*R v HM Treasury, ex parte Smedley* (1985));
   - an individual challenging the executive's treaty-making power in respect of the Treaty on European Union, on the basis that they were a concerned citizen (*R v Secretary of State for Foreign and Commonwealth Affairs, ex parte Rees-Mogg* (1994)); and
   - an individual wishing to challenge the decision of a Health Authority, in this case relating to contraception for girls, since she was the mother of a young daughter (*Gillick v West Norfolk and Wisbeach Area Health Authority* (1986)).

c) Pressure or interest groups

1. Pressure or interest groups may be able to claim sufficient interest if a decision affects their interests or those of their members.

2. Some examples include:
   - an association of taxi operators wishing to challenge a decision to increase the number of taxi licences available (*R v Liverpool Corporation, ex parte Liverpool Taxi Operators' Association* (1972));
   - the Royal College of Nursing wishing to challenge a decision of the Department of Health in respect of the role of nurses in terminations (*Royal College of Nursing v Department of Health and Social Security* (1981)); and
   - the Equal Opportunities Commission wishing to challenge statutory provisions that discriminated against female employees (*R v Employment Secretary, ex parte EOC* (1995)).

3. The granting of sufficient interest for pressure or interest groups in respect of matters that affect society as a whole has been a more complex issue.

4. In *R v Secretary of State for the Environment, ex parte Rose Theatre Trust Company Ltd* (1990) the court found that the group, formed to save Shakespeare's Rose Theatre from being built upon, did not have sufficient interest; their mere assertion of an interest did not suffice.

5. However, the court has taken a more inclusive or liberal approach in cases since. For example:

   - *R v Poole Borough Council, ex parte BeeBee* (1991) – the court ruled that the World Wildlife Fund had sufficient interest to challenge the decision to grant planning permission for the development of land of special scientific interest.

   - *R v Inspectorate of Pollution, ex parte Greenpeace Ltd (No. 2)* (1994) – the court held that Greenpeace had sufficient interest to challenge the decision in respect of the location of a nuclear processing plant. This was because it was a large organisation with the prime objective of protecting the environment; had members residing within the area; and had invested both money and expertise so a properly mounted challenge could be made. It was therefore in the public interest to grant Greenpeace sufficient interest.

   - *R v Secretary of State for Foreign and Commonwealth Affairs, ex parte World Development Movement* (1995) – the court held that the WDM had sufficient interest to challenge the decision to grant financial aid to Malaysia for the building of the Pergau dam. The WDM had considerable expertise in the matter of providing such aid and, the court emphasised, there was no other means of challenging the decision.

d) Individuals claiming for judicial review for a breach of human rights under the Human Rights Act 1998

1. A new test of sufficient interest was created by the Human Rights Act 1998. Under s 7 of the Act a claim can only be brought by a 'victim' of an alleged breach of Convention rights.

2. Pressure or interest groups do not have sufficient interest unless they can establish that one or more of their actual members are, in fact, a 'victim'.

11.6 Remedies

1. Generally there are two types of remedy applied for in cases of judicial review: prerogative orders and, under private law, the remedies of declarations, injunctions and damages.

2. All remedies are granted at the **discretion** of the court. Thus a remedy may be refused, even when the applicant has established their case when:
   - there has been a delay in commencing proceedings;
   - the applicant has acted unreasonably; and/or
   - where the public interest of ensuring efficient administration would be harmed.

3. Application can be made for more than one remedy and the court has the discretion to order any of the remedies in combination, or an alternative one to that actually applied for: s 31(4) Supreme Court Act 1981.

11.6.1 The Prerogative Orders (CPR 1998 r 54.2)

These orders cannot be used against the Crown. However, they can be issued against individual Ministers.

1. **Quashing Orders** (previously an order of *certiorari*)
   This quashes or sets aside the original decision and therefore acts retrospectively. Where only part of a decision is *ultra vires* that part can be severed and quashed whilst the rest of the decision stands.

2. **Mandatory Orders** (previously orders of *mandamus*)
   This orders the body to act and if it then fails to do so the body will be in contempt of court.

3. **Prohibiting Orders** (previously orders of *prohibition*)
   This prevents the body from making a decision that would, if it made it, be susceptible to a quashing order. In other words this order acts prospectively in that it prevents a body acting *ultra vires* in the future. Failure to comply with such an order will amount to a contempt of court.

11.6.2 Private law remedies

1. Declaration

This is a statement of the legal position of the parties so in this sense is not in the full sense a remedy. Declarations cannot be enforced but it is unlikely that a body would ignore one. In contrast to prerogative orders, a declaration can be made against the Crown.

2. Injunction

This restrains a body or person from doing something unlawful (a negative injunction) or orders them to undo something that was done unlawfully (a positive injunction). Injunctions may also be interim or permanent.

Injunctions cannot be issued against the Crown. They can be issued against an individual Minister but only as an action of last resort: *M v Home Office* (1993). If such a Minister fails to comply with the injunction they may be held in contempt of court.

3. Damages

A claim for damages must be attached to a claim for one of the other remedies above (CPR 1998 r 54.3(2)). Damages will only be awarded though where they would have been granted if the action had been a private law action.

11.6.3 Remedies and the Human Rights Act 1998

1. Section 8 of the Act provides for the court to award a remedy or 'make such order within its jurisdiction as it considers just and appropriate'.
2. Section 12(4) provides that in the case of an injunction, the court is to have particular regard to the right of freedom of expression.
3. Damages will not be awarded unless the court is satisfied they are necessary. Damages cannot be claimed against the courts, except where a judicial body has been in breach of right to liberty (Article 5 ECHR).
4. Damages cannot be awarded against Parliament – instead a declaration of incompatibility should be made: see Chapter 9.

CHAPTER 12

The Grounds for Judicial Review

ILLEGALITY (acting *ultra vires*)

- narrow or simple *ultra vires*
- errors of law and/or errors of fact
- wide *ultra vires*, including

  ✓ improper purpose
  ✓ relevant and irrelevant considerations
  ✓ unauthorised delegation
  ✓ fettering discretion
  ✓ failure to act
  ✓ failing to comply with ECHR rights

IRRATIONALITY (acting unreasonably)

- *Wednesbury* unreasonableness
- unreasonable or onerous conditions
- proportionality (HRA 1998)

PROCEDURAL IMPROPRIETY (acting unfairly)

- statutory procedural requirements
- rules of natural justice/ Article 6 ECHR, including

  ✓ right to a fair hearing
  ✓ the rule against bias
  ✓ failure to give reasons

- legitimate expectation

12.1 Classifying the grounds for judicial review

1. It is extremely difficult to classify the grounds for judicial review since they are broad and can overlap. This was recognised by the House of Lords in *Boddington v British Transport Police* (1998).
2. A useful starting point is the classification in *Council for Civil Service Unions v Minister for the Civil Service* (1985) (the *GCHQ* Case) where Lord Diplock referred to the following three grounds:
   - **illegality**;
   - **irrationality** (or **unreasonableness**); and
   - **procedural impropriety**.
3. However, Lord Diplock recognised that these grounds may overlap and that others may be developed to supplement them.
4. Grounds that have developed since include:
   - **proportionality**, particularly since the passing of the Human Rights Act 1998;
   - a new means of acting unlawfully, by **contravening s 6 of the HRA 1998**; and
   - **legitimate expectation**.
5. The table at the start of this chapter should therefore be used as a guide in identifying the grounds for judicial review, and is based on the three grounds in the *GCHQ* Case.

12.2 Illegality

12.2.1 Narrow or simple *ultra vires*

1. A body will act in this way when it acts outside of the powers conferred on it: in other words it lacks the necessary jurisdiction.

2. Lord Diplock in the *GCHQ* Case defined this as where 'the decision maker must understand correctly the law that regulates his decision making power and give effect to it'.

3. Examples of bodies acting in such a way include:

- *Attorney-General v Fulham Corporation* (1921) – in this case statute granted local authorities the power to provide a washhouse for local people. The Corporation interpreted this as granting it the power to provide a laundry service. According to the court this was unlawful because a washhouse was where someone did their own laundry.

- *Bromley London Borough Council v Greater London Council* (1983) – the House of Lords held that an obligation on the GLC to provide an 'efficient and economic' public transport service did not give the Council the power to subsidise the London Underground for social reasons.

- *R v Lord Chancellor, ex parte Witham* (1998) – the Lord Chancellor, under the Supreme Court Act 1981, removed the exemption for payment of court fees for litigants receiving income support. The court found that the Act did not expressly provide for the removal of access to justice and hence the Lord Chancellor had acted *ultra vires*.

- In contrast, in *Akumah v Hackney London Borough Council* (2005) the House of Lords held that the Council had statutory power to manage, regulate and control 'dwelling houses' and this should be interpreted widely to include regulation of car parking. Consequently the Council's action to clamp cars in a car park attached to a block of flats was held *intra vires*.

12.2.2 Errors of law and/or errors of fact

1. An error of law can take several forms including incorrect interpretation, whether discretion has been properly

exercised, and whether irrelevant considerations have been considered or relevant ones ignored.

2. Generally all errors of law are reviewable: *Anisiminic Ltd v Foreign Compensation Commission* (1969) and *R v Lord President of the Privy Council, ex parte Page* (1992).

3. Examples of bodies acting in such a way include:
   - *Perilly v Tower Hamlets Borough Council* (1973) – the Council had misinterpreted the law so instead of granting stall licences only in order of application, it could grant a licence to the son of a deceased licence holder.
   - *R v Secretary of State for the Home Department, ex parte Venables* (1998) – the Home Secretary was held to have misdirected himself as to the law when increasing the tariff for two young murderers on the basis they should be treated as adults.

4. Errors of fact are not usually reviewable unless they are central to the decision that has been made, for example:
   - if the decision is based on facts for which there is no evidence (*Ashbridge Investments v Minister of Housing and Local Government* (1965)); and
   - where facts are proved incorrect or have been ignored or misunderstood (*R v Criminal Injuries Compensation Board, ex parte A* (1992)).

5. Where the decision involves a person's individual rights, the courts are more likely to review any error of fact. For example, in *R v Secretary of State for the Home Department, ex parte Khawaja* (1984) the court held that whether the applicant was indeed an illegal immigrant had to be determined as fact before the power to detain or expel could be exercised.

12.2.3 Wide *ultra vires*

1. These various grounds are concerned with the way in which bodies exercise their discretion; regardless of how wide a body's discretion may be, the court can examine

whether it has been exercised *ultra vires*. *Padfield v Minister for Agriculture, Fisheries and Food* (1968).

A. Improper purpose

1. This is where the body uses its powers to achieve a purpose that it is not empowered to do.
2. Examples of the application of this ground include:
   - *R v Secretary of State for Foreign and Commonwealth Affairs, ex parte World Development Movement* (1995) – where the court held that the Minister had acted unlawfully by granting aid to Malaysia because it did not promote development of the country's economy, as required by statute.
   - *Porter v Magill* (2002) – the House of Lords ruled that the power of local authorities to sell property to tenants was unlawfully used to secure electoral votes.

B. Relevant and irrelevant considerations

1. In exercising its discretion a body must be seen to take into account all relevant considerations and not to be swayed in its decision-making by irrelevant ones. It should be noted that this can overlap with the previous ground of improper purpose.
2. In *R v Somerset County Council, ex parte Fewings* (1995) three types of considerations were identified:
   - considerations that must be taken into account and which are therefore mandatory;
   - considerations that must not be taken into account and which are therefore prohibited; and
   - discretionary considerations that a decision-maker may have regard to, in which case the court will only intervene if it believes the decision-maker has acted unreasonably.
3. Examples of the application of this ground include:
   - *Wheeler v Leicester City Council* (1985) – the decision of a local authority to refuse to permit a local rugby club to use its playing field was found to have been based on the irrelevant consideration that the club had failed to

prevent some of its members from touring South Africa during the apartheid regime.

- *R v Talbot Borough Council, ex parte Jones* (1988) – the decision to grant priority housing to a divorced councillor was decided on the basis of irrelevant factors with relevant ones, such as the needs of other applicants on the waiting list, ignored.
- *R v Secretary of State for the Home Department, ex parte Venables* (1997) – the Secretary of State, when reviewing the tariff of child murderers, took into account the irrelevant consideration of public opinion. In *R (Bulger) v Secretary of State* (2001) it was also concluded that the Home Secretary had failed to take into account the relevant considerations of the progress and development of the children whilst in detention.
- *R v Liverpool Crown Court, ex parte Luxury Leisure* (1998) – the court found that the local authority had acted on the basis of relevant considerations when it had considered its knowledge of the area and community when deciding to create a system of permits for amusement arcades.
- *R v Gloucestershire County Council, ex parte Barry* (1997) – a local authority, when exercising its statutory obligation to provide care for disabled persons, could take into account its financial resources as a relevant consideration in determining how to meet those needs (see also *R v Sefton Metropolitan Borough Council, ex parte Help the Aged* (1997)).

C. Unauthorised delegation

1. Where powers are conferred under statute they should generally be exercised by the body on which they are conferred, and should not be delegated in an unauthorised manner to another body or person.
2. Delegation by a Minister to the personnel in their Department is not considered unauthorised delegation: *Carltona v Works Commissioner* (1943). For example, in *R v Secretary of State for the Home Department, ex parte*

Oladehinde (1991) the court held that decisions in respect of deportation could be legally delegated to an Immigration Inspector.

3. Examples of the application of this ground include:
   - *Barnard v National Dock Labour Board* (1953) – the decision to delegate power of the London Dock Board to a port manager was unauthorised and hence illegal.
   - *R v Talbot Borough Council, ex parte Jones* (1988) – the power to allocate council housing had been delegated to an officer when the power to make such decisions rested in the hands of the chair of the housing committee.

D. Fettering discretion

1. This occurs when the decision-maker binds themselves to exercise their discretion in a particular way, sometimes by imposing a rigid rule, so that they are no longer able to exercise discretion in individual cases; where decision-makers have discretion it should be exercised in each case according to its merits: *British Oxygen Co v Board of Trade* (1971).

2. Some examples of the application of this ground include:
   - *Sagnata Investments v Norwich Corporation* (1971) – the policy adopted by the Corporation of not granting any licences for amusement arcades resulted in it failing to consider any cases on their merits.
   - *R v Army Board of the Defence Council, ex parte Anderson* (1992) – the Army Board's policy of never permitting oral hearings amounted to an unlawful fettering of discretion.
   - *R v Chief Constable of North Wales Police, ex parte AB* (1997) – the decision to publicly disclose information pertaining to a convicted paedophile was held to have been based on the merits of the case and was not the adoption of any policy on behalf of the police.
   - *R v Secretary of State for the Home Department, ex parte Simms* (1999) – the Home Secretary's blanket policy of not permitting professionals to visit prisoners (such as journalists) was held unlawful.

E. Failure to act

1. This is where a body has a statutory duty to act and fails to do so. Whether the duty to act is enforceable by the courts will depend on the wording of the statute: if the obligation to act is clear and precise the court will hold it enforceable. Conversely, if the duty is not specific the court will not hold it enforceable.

2. If, under statute, the Secretary of State has default powers to intervene to ensure the duty to act takes place, the courts will generally not intervene: *R v Secretary of State for the Environment, ex parte Norwich City Council* (1982).

F. Failing to comply with ECHR rights

1. Acting unlawfully also includes failing to abide by Convention rights, contrary to s 6 HRA 1998. Judicial review will lie against the authority committing the alleged breach (see Chapter 9).

12.3 Irrationality

12.3.1 Irrationality or *Wednesbury* unreasonableness

1. This ground is also referred to as **unreasonableness**. It is a far wider and vaguer ground for judicial review than illegality. Consequently this ground is one where the court comes far closer to examining the merits of the decision. It is because of this that the courts will generally only accept this ground if a high level of unreasonableness is found and such cases are rare.

2. This is seen in the case of *Associated Picture Houses Ltd v Wednesbury Corporation* (1948), in which the court stated that it would only interfere where a decision was 'so unreasonable that no reasonable authority could ever have come to it'.

3. In the *GCHQ* Case, Lord Diplock referred to this ground as operating only when a decision has no rational basis or

'is so outrageous in its denial of accepted moral standards that no sensible person who has applied his mind to the question to be decided could have arrived at it'.

4. For example, in *Brind v Secretary of State for the Home Department* (1991) a ban on live media interviews with supporters of the IRA was held not to be unreasonable; it was a rational means of preventing terrorists gaining publicity.

5. However, if there is interference with a person's human rights the court will require a higher justification before it will consider the decision to be reasonable: *R v Ministry of Defence, ex parte Smith* (1996).

6. For example, in *R (Rogers) v Swindon NHS Primary Care Trust* (2006) the court found that the decision of the Trust to grant certain breast cancer treatment only in 'exceptional personal or clinical circumstances' to be irrational, particularly since it had the necessary funds to provide such treatment.

12.3.2 Unreasonable or onerous conditions

1. A decision may be unreasonable if conditions are attached to it, which are difficult or impossible to perform: *Pyx Granite Co. Ltd v Ministry of Housing and Local Government* (1958).

12.3.3 Proportionality

1. The requirement to act proportionally means that powers must be exercised in a manner that is proportionate to the objective pursued: in other words, no more than is necessary.

2. Originally the English courts did not accept proportionality as a ground for judicial review: *Brind* (above).

3. Over time, however, the courts appeared more willing to adopt the concept: see, for example, Lord Diplock's comments in the *GCHQ* Case (above) and *R v Chief Constable of Sussex, ex parte International Trader's Ferry Ltd* (1999).

4. The need for proportionality is now accepted in the context of decisions impacting on Convention rights as a result of the passing of the Human Rights Act 1998. This is because it is a doctrine favoured by the European Court of Human Rights, and s 2 of the Act requires the jurisprudence of the Court to be taken into account.

5. An example of the application of proportionality can be seen in *R (Daly) v Secretary of State for the Home Department* (2001). In this case the House of Lords held the policy of permitting the scrutiny of a prisoner's legal correspondence to not be a proportionate means of achieving any objective in the public interest.

6. In *Daly*, the House of Lords provided a three-part test to examining the proportionality of a measure:
   - whether the objective is sufficiently important to justify limiting a fundamental right;
   - whether the measures taken are designed to meet the objective and rationally connected to it; and
   - whether the means used are no more than is necessary to achieve the objective.

   The House of Lords also stressed that in cases involving a human rights element, proportionality was the standard of review that should be applied.

7. The courts have indicated that proportionality extends beyond human rights cases: see for example *R (Alconbury Developments Ltd) v Secretary of State for the Environment, Transport and the Regions* (2001). In this case Lord Slynn argued for proportionality to become a separate fourth ground for judicial review (see also *Rehman v Secretary of State for the Home Department* (2003)).

8. At present, the two tests, *Wednesbury* unreasonableness and proportionality, can be applied, with the acknowledgment that cases involving human rights must use proportionality. The courts have recognised the co-existence of the tests: see *R (Association of British Civilian Internees: Far East Region) v Secretary of State for Defence* (2003) and *R (Ann Summers Ltd) v Jobcentre Plus* (2003).

9. However, the courts have also recognised the increasing significance of proportionality and the possible eventual disappearance of *Wednesbury* unreasonableness in the future.

12.4 Procedural impropriety

1. Lord Diplock in the *GCHQ* Case (above) described this ground of judicial review as including 'the failure to observe basic rules of natural justice or failure to act with procedural fairness' and also 'failure ... to observe procedural rules expressly laid down in ... legislative instrument'.

12.4.1 Statutory procedural requirements

1. Failure to comply with a procedural requirement set out in statute could render a decision *ultra vires* and hence void. Such procedural requirements could include, for example:
   - time limits;
   - consultations;
   - providing specific information; and
   - providing notice.
2. The courts have traditionally distinguished between rules that are mandatory and those that are discretionary. This is ascertained by examining the statute. Failure to comply with a mandatory requirement will render a decision void; failure to abide by a discretionary requirement may not invalidate the decision.
3. However, more recently the courts have been less inclined to make a distinction on such a basis: see *London and Clydeside Estates Ltd v Aberdeen DC* (1980) and *R v Immigration Appeal Tribunal, ex parte Jeyeanthen* (2000). Whether the decision is invalid therefore depends on the facts of the case and the nature of the particular procedural requirement.

4. Examples of the application of this ground include:
   - *Ridge v Baldwin* (1964) – regulations under the Police Act 1964 required a formal inquiry before a chief constable could be dismissed, hence failure to do so rendered the dismissal invalid.
   - *Bradbury v Enfield London Borough Council* (1967) – failure to give notice on the closing of schools and the creation of new ones invalidated the decision since it was a requirement under the Education Act 1944.
   - *Agricultural, Horticultural and Forestry Industry Training Board v Aylesbury Mushrooms Ltd* (1972) – when making a decision the respective Minister had failed to consult the Mushroom Growers Association, which was held to be a breach of a statutory duty to consultation.

12.4.2 The rules of natural justice

1. The origin of these rules of procedure is found in the **common law**. They effectively require the body to act fairly.
2. With the passing of the HRA 1998, Article 6 of the Convention, which requires 'a fair and public hearing within a reasonable time by an independent and impartial tribunal established by law', is now enforceable in English courts.

A. The right to a fair hearing (*audi alteram partem*)

1. Traditionally the courts would only apply the right to a fair hearing to judicial decisions: *Local Government Board v Arlidge* (1915).
2. In *Ridge v Baldwin* (1964), however, it was concluded that irrespective of whether a decision is judicial or administrative there is, in principle, a right to be heard. Judicial proceedings will attract a higher procedural standard of the right to a fair hearing than administrative decisions.
3. One exception to the right to be heard is where there are overriding factors in the interests of national security:

GCHQ Case (above). (See also *R v Secretary of State for Transport, ex parte Pegasus Holdings Ltd* (1989).)

4. Failure to permit a hearing may also not invalidate the decision when the court concludes that the outcome of the decision would have been the same regardless. For example, in *Glynn v Keele University* (1971) the court dismissed an application by a student against their expulsion from the university on the basis that no representation by them would have affected the decision.

5. Whether a hearing is itself fair is not subject to fixed requirements, although the more serious the consequences for the individual, the higher the standard required for the hearing to be fair.

6. A fair hearing could require one or more of the following requirements therefore, depending on the facts of the case:
   - notification of a hearing/ advance notice;
   - to be informed of the case against;
   - the opportunity to respond to evidence;
   - an oral hearing;
   - legal representation; and
   - the ability to question witnesses.

7. For example, there is no absolute right to an oral hearing. According to *R v Army Board of the Defence Council, ex parte Anderson* (1992), whether an oral hearing is required for the hearing to be fair will depend on the subject-matter and circumstances of the particular case. Consequently the question is whether any written proceedings are sufficient to ensure a fair hearing.

8. The right to cross-examine any witnesses will only arise if there is an oral hearing.

9. Similarly, the right to legal representation will depend on the nature of the hearing and the rights that will be affected. In *R v Secretary of State for the Home Department, ex parte Tarrant* (1985) the criteria to be applied in determining whether legal representation is necessary include:

- the seriousness of the charge and potential penalty;
- whether any points of law are likely to be raised;
- the ability of the person to present their own case;
- the complexity of the procedure to be applied; and
- whether there is need for reasonable speed in making the decision.

B. The rule against bias (*nemo judex in causa sua*)

1. Impartial and independent decision-making is a fundamental aspect of the rule of law (see Chapter 3).

2. The rule against bias is described as being strict in that the risk or appearance of bias will suffice. As stated by Lord Hewart in *R v Sussex Justices, ex parte McCarthy* (1924) 'justice must not only be done but must manifestly and undoubtedly be seen to be done'.

3. If a decision-maker becomes aware that they may be biased, they should remove themselves from the decision-making process: *AWG Group v Morrison* (2006).

4. A financial interest, however small, will automatically indicate bias: *Dimes v Grand Junction Canal Co.* (1952) and *Metropolitan Properties Co. v Lannon* (1969).

5. This principle, of automatic disqualification because of a direct interest, was extended in *R v Bow Street Metropolitan and Stipendiary Magistrate, ex parte Pinochet Ugarte* (1999).

6. In this case extradition proceedings were challenged on the basis that Lord Hoffman had links with Amnesty International, which had provided evidence. Whilst there was no evidence of actual bias, it was concluded that there could be the appearance of bias and therefore the case was re-heard. The House of Lords stated that any direct interest whether financial, proprietary or otherwise would lead to automatic disqualification.

7. In other instances, where there is no direct personal interest but a non-direct interest that may give the appearance of bias, the court will examine whether in the view of a 'fair minded and informed observer' taking into account all the circumstances there is a 'real possibility' of bias: *Porter v*

Magill (2002). This test was confirmed by the House of Lords in *Lawal v Northern Spirit* (2003) and *Gillies v Secretary of State for Work and Pensions* (2006).

C. Failure to give reasons

1. Numerous statutes impose a duty to provide reasons. For example, there is a duty to give reasons on request on tribunals and public inquiries: Tribunals and Inquiries Act 1992.

2. There is no absolute duty to give reasons under the common law rules of natural justice, although there is a strong presumption that they should be provided: *R v Secretary of State for the Home Department, ex parte Doody* (1993).

3. There have been developments in the common law though where reasons must be provided. These include for example:
   - where decisions are analogous to those of a judicial body: *R v Civil Service Appeal Board, ex parte Cunningham* (1991) and *R v Ministry of Defence, ex parte Murray* (1998).
   - where the decisions involve very important interests so that the individual would be at a clear disadvantage if reasons were not provided. For example, in *ex parte Doody* (above) reasons were required as the applicant otherwise had no knowledge of the case against them; the decision at hand was the fixing of a minimum sentence for a life prisoner (see also *Stefan v General Medical Council* (1999)). In *R v Secretary of State for the Home Department, ex parte Fayed* (1997) the court ruled that some indication of the Home Secretary's objections to the application for a British passport should have been given; and
   - where the decision is unusual or a severe penalty can be applied. For example, in *R v DPP ex parte Manning* (2000) reasons should have been provided for the decision not to prosecute after a coroner's finding of unlawful killing.

4. Conversely, there are situations where there will be no duty to provide reasons. This may occur where to do so would be extremely costly or particularly onerous on the decision-maker: see *R v Higher Education Funding Council, ex parte Institute of Dental Surgery* (1994) and *R (Asha Foundation) v Millennium Commission* (2003).

5. Where a Minister fails to provide reasons for a decision, the court may infer that there were in fact no proper reasons for that decision: *Padfield v Minister of Agriculture, Fisheries and Food* (1968).

6. Where reasons are required, they must enable the parties to understand the basis for the decision, but this does not necessarily mean they have to be detailed or comprehensive. The level of detail necessary will depend on the facts of the case: *South Buckinghamshire DC v Porter* (2004).

7. Article 6 of the ECHR does not explicitly require the giving of reasons. However, it could be implied because of the need to have reasons in order to be able to exercise any right to appeal. Article 5 of the Convention, however, expressly states in the context of the right to liberty and security that arrested persons shall be informed promptly and in a language they understand of the reasons for their arrest (see Chapter 10).

12.4.3 Legitimate expectation

1. Legitimate expectation is a well accepted principle of EC law, and has been increasingly recognised by the English courts. It occurs when the decision-maker, by either their words or actions, creates a reasonable and therefore legitimate expectation that certain procedures will be followed in reaching a decision.

2. If such expectations have been created, the decision-maker is not able to ignore them when coming to a decision on the matter unless there are good reasons not to do so: *R (Nadarajah) v Secretary of State for the Home Department, R*

(Abdi) v Secretary of State for the Home Department (2005).

3. Whether a legitimate expectation has been created will depend on the circumstances. According to Lord Diplock in the *GCHQ* Case (above) a legitimate expectation may arise in two circumstances:
   - from either an **express promise** given on behalf of the decision-maker; or
   - from the existence of a **regular practice** that the applicant can reasonably expect to continue.

4. For a promise to create a legitimate expectation it must be clear, unambiguous and precise: *R v Inland Revenue Commissioners, ex parte MFK Underwriting Agents Ltd* (1990). However, the individual does not have to be aware of it, since it is the decision-maker that should be aware of any expectation created: *R (Rashid) v Secretary of State for the Home Department* (2005).

5. Some examples of where there was a clear, unambiguous and precise promise, creating a legitimate expectation, include:
   - *R v Liverpool Corporation, ex parte Liverpool Taxi Fleet Operators Association* (1972) – the Corporation had given an express representation that licences would not be revoked without prior consultation. This created a legitimate expectation which could be relied on when the Corporation then failed to carry out that consultation.
   - *Attorney-General for Hong Kong v Ng Yuen Shiu* (1983) – it was concluded that an illegal immigrant had a legitimate expectation of an interview prior to deportation and for his case to be considered on its individual merits because of an express undertaking given by the British Government.
   - *R v Secretary of State for the Home Department, ex parte Asif Mahmood Khan* (1984) – the issuing of a circular providing the criteria under which a child would be permitted entry into the UK was held to have created a legitimate expectation that those criteria would be applied.

- *R v (Bibi) v Newham LBC* (2001) – it was held that promises made by the local authority had created a legitimate expectation that the applicants (refugees) would be provided with accommodation with security of tenure.

6. Examples of where the promise was not considered sufficiently clear, unambiguous and precise enough to create a legitimate expectation include:

   - *R v Secretary of State for the Home Department, ex parte Behluli* (1998) – the applicant argued that in the case of their expulsion they had a legitimate expectation that the Dublin Convention be applied. The court held that the statements being relied upon did not create a sufficiently clear intention on behalf of the government to create a legitimate expectation.

   - *R v DPP, ex parte Kebilene* (1999) – four applicants sought to rely on a legitimate expectation that the DPP would exercise their discretion to prosecute only in accordance with the ECHR. They based their argument on the ratification of the Convention by the government; the enactment of the Human Rights Act 1998; and from public statements made by Ministers. However, the Act whilst passed had not yet come into force. The court concluded that no legitimate expectation had been created.

   - *R v Secretary of State for Education and Employment, ex parte Begbie* (2000) – a Labour Party pre-election promise that children benefiting from the assisted-places scheme would continue to receive this until the end of their education was held not to create a legitimate expectation. This was because Labour was in opposition at the time the statement was made and could not know of all the complexities of the matter until in office; consequently the promise was unclear. Thus, as a consequence of this decision, a pre-election promise cannot bind a new government.

7. It should be noted that a legitimate expectation cannot arise from a promise or representation that is illegal: *R v Ministry of Agriculture, Fisheries and Food, ex parte Hamble (Offshore) Fisheries Ltd* (1995) and *R (Bibi) v Newham LBC* (2001).

8. The question of whether there is an enforceable legitimate expectation is more complex when it involves a situation where there has been a change of policy.

9. Whilst legitimate expectation as a ground for judicial review promotes certainty and trust in executive authority, thus upholding the rule of law, it must also be recognised that the executive must be able to develop, adapt and change policies particularly if in the public interest.

10. In *R v North and East Devon Health Authority, ex parte Coughlan* (1999) the Court of Appeal identified three such situations involving legitimate expectation:

(a) Where a body changes policy, it should consider previous policy and representations made, before changing that policy. Thereafter, in cases of claims of legitimate expectation, review will take place on the basis of whether the decision is *Wednesbury* unreasonable (see above).

   Example

   ● *R v Secretary of State for the Home Department, ex parte Hargreaves* (1996) – there was an agreement between prisoners and prison authorities that, subject to good behaviour, prisoners could apply for home leave after serving one third of their sentence. The Home Secretary then changed this to having served half of the sentence. The court held that the agreement did not give rise to a legitimate expectation and that in any case the Home Secretary's change of policy was reasonable.

(b) If there is a legitimate expectation of being consulted prior to a decision, the court will examine closely any change in that policy to ensure that any decision is made fairly.

(c) Where undertakings by a decision-maker create a substantive legitimate expectation, the court will very closely examine any change of policy. The court will balance carefully the interests of fairness given the individual's legitimate expectation against any overriding need to change the policy in the public interest.

Examples

- *R v Secretary of State for Health, ex parte US Tobacco International Inc.* (1992) – the company, using a government grant, opened a factory in 1985 producing snuff. In 1988 the government was provided with additional evidence of the health risks of snuff and decided to ban it. It was held that whilst there was a legitimate expectation created by the government's prior actions, that expectation could not override the need to change the policy in the public interest.

- *R v North and East Devon Health Authority, ex parte Coughlan* (1999) – the applicant lived in a home for the severely disabled and had been told by the Health Authority that it would be her home for life. She was then informed that the home was to be closed and she would be transferred. The court held that a legitimate expectation had been created, which no public-interest factor could override.

Index